THE CONFIDENCE QUOTIENT

10 STEPS TO CONQUER SELF-DOUBT

**MERYLE GELLMAN, Ph.D.
and DIANE GAGE**

Foreword by Og Mandino

WORLD ALMANAC PUBLICATIONS NEW YORK, NEW YORK

DEDICATION

To Larry Gellman, whose love is never less than a commitment. To Gregg and Brendan Gellman, who fill all the spaces in my heart and simply light up my life.

MG

To Gene, who supports me in all I do. And to George & Charlotte Coleman, who gave me the confidence I needed to try, and to Kathleen White and Karen Coleman, who always cheer me on.

DG

Interior and cover design: Nancy Bumpus
Copyright © 1985 by Meryle Gellman and Diane Gage
All rights reserved. No part of this book may be reproduced in any form or by any means without permission in writing from the publisher.
First published in 1985.
Distributed in the United States
by Ballantine Books, a division of Random House, Inc.
and in Canada by Random House of Canada, Ltd.
Library of Congress Catalog Card Number:85-051282
Newspaper Enterprise Association ISBN 0-911818-91-X
Ballantine Books ISBN 0-345-32662-8
The authors are grateful to Farrar, Straus & Giroux, Inc. for permission to quote from Madeline L'Engle's A Circle of Quiet, Copyright © 1972 by Madeline L'Engle Franklin.
Printed in the United States of America
World Almanac Publications
Newspaper Enterprise Association
A division of United Media Enterprises
A Scripps Howard company
200 Park Avenue
New York, NY 10166
10 9 8 7 6 5 4 3 2 1

STILLMEADOW CENTER
833 South Fourth Street
Springfield, Illinois 62703

THE CONFIDENCE QUOTIENT

10 STEPS TO CONQUER SELF-DOUBT

CONTENTS

Acknowledgments vi
Foreword by Og Mandino vii
Introduction x
Preface xi
 1 Self-Doubt: A Love/Hate Relationship 1
 2 Blueprints from the Past 9
 3 Be Your Own Therapist: A 10-Step Plan
   to Conquer Self-Doubt 19
 4 Housewife Syndrome 49
 5 Self-Doubt on the Job 63
 6 "Marriage Will Make Me Happy" and
   Other Myths 71
 7 Little Ones Can Have Big Fears: Help
   for Children and Teens 85
 8 How Jealousy and Envy Affect
   Self-Esteem 95
 9 Alcoholism, Drug Abuse, Weight Gain:
   The Symptoms or the Cause? 103
10 Be All You Can Be: Conquering the Fear
   of Failure and the Fear of Success 113
Afterword 122
Footnotes 126
Index 127

ACKNOWLEDGMENTS

This book wouldn't have been possible without the support I received from many wonderful people. I extend my thanks and appreciation to: Mom, Dad and Jerry for letting me know that the prize is in the effort, no matter what the outcome; Betty and Norm and Paul and Dorothy for helping to create a man who can nourish and respect the integrity of my unfolding and separate self; Wendy, for always seeing my potential; my agent, Stan, for being such a mensch and for teaching me that the publishing world can be an ethical one; agent Bill Gladstone for believing in this project and believing in me; our publisher Jane Flatt and editor Rob Fitz, for their excitement and enthusiasm about this book; my clients, for trusting me enough to share their complex and special worlds; and finally Diane Gage for how she can take my thoughts and words and make them sing.

Meryle Gellman

My deepest gratitude to Kathleen White, for her thoughtful insights that became such a meaningful part of this book. My thanks to the following individuals, who shared their special talents with me and made my work easier: George and Charlotte Coleman, Gene Gage, Marcia Hibsch, Leslie Leupold, Linda O'Neill, Karen Pecor, Sue Schudson, and Sandra Brooks. My appreciation to: Literary Agent Bill Gladstone, for suggesting the project to me; Literary Agent Stan Corwin, for making it a reality; Rob Fitz, for his graceful editing; and Jane Flatt for her commitment to the project. And my special thanks to Meryle Gellman, for recognizing the need for this book and entrusting me to help her write it. Her energy and determination are an inspiration to all of us.

Diane Gage

FOREWORD

One morning several years ago, I rushed out to my garage, late for an appointment. I turned the ignition key in my convertible. Nothing. I turned it again. Still nothing. Could it be the battery? I flipped the headlight switch and lights glared brightly. I turned on the radio and heard the voice of my favorite morning talk show host. I tried the windshield wiper blades and they bounced back and forth in unison. It couldn't be the battery, could it?

I went back into the house and phoned my mechanic, describing the sorry circumstances. I could hear him chuckling. "Sir," he asked, "didn't we install a burglar alarm in that car a couple of months ago?"

"You did."

"Well, you've probably tripped the kill switch."

"What's the 'kill switch'?" I asked, trying to keep my temper.

"That alarm is set up," he said, "so that after you lock your car you insert that funny shaped key into the slot in the fender, turn it, and the system is activated. Then, if anyone tries to break in, a siren under the hood will sound and hopefully scare off the would-be thief."

"All that I know. So what's a kill switch?"

"It's part of the alarm system. Just a small toggle switch. You flip that on before you get out of your car, lock it, and turn on the burglar alarm. Then if someone is still foolish enough to try to break into your car after the siren has started blaring, they won't be able to jump the wires and drive off with the automobile because the kill switch has cut off all current going to the starter. Don't you remember?"

"No, I don't. I was never told about any kill switch and I certainly have never used it. I don't even know where it is."

"Sir, we don't install that switch out in the open. We try to hide it—under the dashboard or under the carpet somewhere. I'll tell you what: I'll send someone out to help you."

He did send someone and we located the mysterious "kill switch" beneath the carpet, turned the ignition key, and the car started immediately. Grinning, he handed me the keys and said, "You must have accidentally tripped it with your foot."

Long after he departed, I kept thinking about the incident. As a writer and lecturer on success I am always looking for fresh stories, examples, and analogies to help make the principles of success understandable and meaningful both to my readers and my audiences, and this "kill switch" episode was too powerful to ignore.

All of us, I'm afraid, have a "kill switch" called self-doubt. Maybe our parents were the first to trip it when we were young and one of them made some unthinking statement about our terrible report card. Maybe a coach tripped it when he told us we could forget about making the team because we just didn't have it. Perhaps our boss tripped it when he passed us by in selecting a new assistant. And worst of all, we might trip it ourselves, when we fail at some endeavor.

So what happens after the "kill switch" is tripped in us and self-doubt takes over? The same thing that happened to my automobile. In my car, the lights still worked, the radio played, the windshield wipers danced . . . but the motor refused to start and there was no forward progress. And here we are, day after day, involved in all sorts of "busy work," making all kinds of motions, perhaps fooling the world and even ourselves that we are active and productive, while all the time we are making not a single inch of forward progress. Self-doubt, that terrible but curable disease, is working as effectively at holding us back as the "kill switch" did in my car.

The Confidence Quotient is an excellent book—wise, understanding, and full of help. Dr. Gellman has managed to avoid all the psychiatric and sociological jargon that does nothing but confuse us in so many self-help books and she has focused on the characteristics and symptoms of self-doubt that all of us can recognize . . . because no one is immune to seizures of doubting his own ability and potential. Most important, she has given us a

10-step plan that will gradually, if we follow her advice, help us to understand and rid ourselves of this monster, or at least subdue it, so that we have a much better chance of achieving the worthwhile things in life. Self-doubt, let me repeat, resides in all of us. Superstars, professional athletes, professors, million dollar producers...all have had to deal with this destroyer of dreams, this "kill switch," and it's a never-ending battle. The Confidence Quotient will not only show you how to recognize the evil but how to deal with it . . . and win.

Og Mandino

INTRODUCTION

Writing this book was a challenge—not only because writing is a time-consuming, often frustrating process, but because I could not present the information without first testing it in my own life.

The first test for me came when I sat down to write and stared at blank paper that soon needed to be filled with thoughtful, useful information that would allow Dr. Meryle Gellman to help you tackle the doubts in your life. As most writers will contend, writing and self-doubt are almost synonymous. So before I began writing, I used the 10-step plan to discover my reinforcer—the creative side within me that has the power to mold words into meaningful shapes.

During the months that I spent working with Dr. Gellman to research and write this book, I discovered that creative side. And I learned that success is simply the willingness to try and that mistakes are stepping stones that can strengthen us if we use them to learn from and not to torment ourselves. I realized that how we reacted to events and people in the past cause many of our doubts today. And I discovered that we can use those past experiences to learn how to create the futures we want by drawing upon the reinforcers within us.

I hope this book will help you to put the doubt in your life in perspective and become acquainted with a more powerful resource—your creative, positive side. You have the confidence you need to overcome self-doubt and make dreams realities.

Diane Gage

PREFACE

Self-doubt is one of the most debilitating and wide-spread psychological problems affecting men and women today. It's a feeling of uncertainty or inadequacy that, if uncontrolled, can color every area of our lives. It can destroy our self-image and harm our relationships with our mates, children, friends, employers, employees, and colleagues.

Self-doubt beats us down and creates feelings of anxiety, inadequacy, frustration, jealousy, envy, uncertainty, and fear. It gnaws away at our self-esteem, prevents us from achieving our goals, and leaves us depressed and dissatisfied.

This book includes a 10-step plan that will help you uncover doubts that prevent you from achieving your goals. Examples of how others have used the ten steps to control self-doubt are included to help you understand the intense and varied feelings people experience when doubt overtakes them. You will see how you can put the plan into action to identify your strengths and weaknesses and determine how the positive and negative forces within you can work together for your benefit.

By the time you complete the 10-step plan and other exercises throughout the book, you will know how self-doubt has affected your life in the past and discover its impact on your life today. And you will learn how to develop a creative strategy to mobilize your inner strengths when confronting self-doubt in the future.

You don't have to be afraid of the unknown; you don't have to jeopardize your relationships with others if you choose to change; you don't have to live up to someone else's expectations; you don't have to listen to negative self-talk; and you don't have to react to situations in the same way as you have in the past. When you've finished reading this book, you'll have the resources you need to overcome your doubts and discover new confidence.

Self-doubt is a universal feeling that everyone experiences in varying degrees at one time or another. It's a subconscious critic that tells you why you can't, why you shouldn't, and why you never will. It judges your actions, weighs your decisions, and evaluates your goals.

A small serving of self-doubt can help you make wise choices and sound decisions. But too much self-doubt can turn a positive outlook into a negative one and threaten your success, happiness, and even your physical well-being.

When you experience self-doubt, you probably long for someone you love, trust, or admire to build up your confidence by pointing out your positive qualities and achievements. You may look to others to bring new perspective to the situation and help you to believe in yourself.

It is common to want someone to help you find a way around obstacles that cause you to doubt your worth and abilities. But friends and relatives can't cheer for you on a twenty-four-hour-a-day basis. The only person you can depend on to fill a void of uncertainty in your life is you.

As a psychotherapist, I see the devastating effects self-doubt has on people who are waiting for someone or something to reassure them. Some people come to me depressed because their lives seem purposeless. Others see themselves as failures because they haven't learned to accept their shortcomings and learn from their mistakes. Still others are so dissatisfied that they try to manipulate the people around them in order to feel important and in control. And many who come to me feel trapped by their lifestyles, marriages, families or careers. They're afraid to change because they fear that if they do, others on whom they currently depend will stop loving them.

Thirteen years ago I, too, became caught in the self-doubt trap. I had worked as an elementary school teacher for seven years before my husband and I had our first son. After taking a maternity leave and then substitute teaching for two years, I became depressed when the time came to go back to work full time. I didn't know what I wanted to do, but I didn't want to continue teaching or be a full-time homemaker.

Instead of creating new alternatives, I began to doubt my ability to do anything other than what I had always done. Listening to the advice of well-meaning friends and relatives confused me even more. Some felt I should stay home full time and others pointed out that I'd lose my tenure if I quit teaching.

After months of agonizing, I sought the guidance of a psychologist. She helped me to see that I was doubting the instincts that were telling me it was time to change careers. I was trying to live up to the roles in which everyone else saw me: school teacher and mother.

I realized that I was bored with teaching but that I would feel stifled if I stayed home full time. As the therapist pointed out, those feelings didn't mean I was a poor teacher or an inadequate mother, which was exactly what the doubter inside me was trying to make me believe.

With that insight and the renewed confidence that went with it, I decided to pursue a master's degree in marriage, family, and child counseling. After I completed the program, our second child was born. Because he had a hearing disability, leaving him to go to work was doubly hard. Nevertheless, I persisted, trying to do my best at work, at home, and at school.

Later, when I decided to pursue my doctorate, doubt took hold of me again. Because my husband had a job that allowed him to spend time at home, he was available to drive car pools to school and take the boys to baseball practice. I spent evenings and weekends with the boys, but because I was not in the traditional role, I questioned my value and worth as a mother.

My husband loved being involved in the boys' daily activities—a rare opportunity for a father—but he resented me for spending so much time away from home. His frustration with my new lifestyle made me wonder if I was doing the right thing. But I knew that if I didn't complete my education then, I'd be discontent later.

Eventually, I completed three years of post-gradate work. Now I realize that my personal experience with self-doubt was the hardest lesson I learned. I discovered that I could pursue personal goals and still keep my family intact. And my husband and I learned that we didn't have to agree on everything to respect each other and maintain our marriage.

I chose not to follow other people's advice or try to live up to their expectations—and overcame the doubts that tried to prevent me from accepting new challenges. I found ways to work around obstacles. Maybe I wasn't the model wife, mother, or friend, but I had made time to be with my family. I had created a new, exciting way of life, one that enabled me to help others while allowing me to set my own hours. I had the resources to give more to others because I believed in and was content with myself.

It is my personal experience with self-doubt and the doubts I've helped my clients overcome that first made me want to write this book. But it wasn't until I spoke about self-doubt and housewife syndrome on radio and television talk shows, and was interviewed for newspaper and magazine articles, that I realized how prevalent self-doubt is in our society. I received hundreds of letters and phone calls from people throughout the country who desperately wanted to know more about overcoming self-doubt. Their desire for more information inspired the writing of this book.

Recognizing the signs of self-doubt and avoiding its negative consequences are not easy. I've designed this book to show you how to come face-to-face with and overcome the doubt in your life, because only then can you begin to feel good about your decisions and content with your actions.

Meryle Gellman

1

Self-Doubt: A Love/Hate Relationship

JANET woke up exhausted. She didn't want to go to work. She had tossed and turned all night, worrying how she would ever complete the annual budget for the communications department of the savings and loan company for which she worked.

It had been a big step for Janet to assume the director's role when her predecessor was promoted three months before. At first she considered turning it down, but her husband and friends encouraged her to take it. Now, she told herself, she was in over her head.

The forms and tables on the oversized spread sheets were an unapproachable maze, but she was too embarrassed to ask for help. What would others think of her if she admitted she didn't know how to plan a budget, she asked herself. Anyway, she was sure that even after it was explained to her she wouldn't understand. She had never been good in math—that's why she had majored in communications.

Janet was certain her job was in jeopardy. Dejected, she did not attempt to complete the budget and turned in blank forms. A week later, Janet's boss called her into his office. "I'm disappointed that you didn't do your budget," he said in an irritated voice. "Can you explain why you didn't even attempt to complete the forms?"

Janet's stomach churned and her throat closed. "I guess," she croaked, coughing to find her voice again. "I-I-I guess I just didn't think I could do it."

Janet didn't lose her job that day. Instead she learned an unforgettable lesson. Mr. Michelson had made it clear that Janet could not use doubt as an excuse for not completing a project—not if she wanted to advance. Janet chose to succeed, so she began confronting her doubts. When she was faced with a complicated project, she asked questions. She tackled previously unexplored areas, telling herself that she would learn from new experiences—even if she made mistakes. Slowly, she felt new confidence and began to trust herself more.

Self-doubt is a natural emotion that most of us have experienced at one time or another. It is that subconscious voice that tells us we're "not good enough." It is a conviction that we're inadequate compared to other more "successful" people. It is a critic that judges our past and questions our future. To determine if self-doubt affects your life, take a few moments to answer the questions in the Confidence Quotient (CQ) Quiz. Put a check in the column that most accurately describes how frequently you feel this way.

The scoring for this quiz is simple. Since all of us experience self-doubt at various times in our lives, most of us will be able to answer "Often" or "Sometimes" to at least one of the questions. Therefore, if you answered "Often" or "Sometimes" to *between 1 and 3* of the questions, your level of self-doubt is quite low and certainly well within the range that would be considered "normal."

If you responded with an "Often" or "Sometimes" to *between 4 and 7* of the questions, you are experiencing moderate levels of self-doubt— not, perhaps, abnormally, but certainly a cause for concern.

If you answered "Often" or "Sometimes" to 8 or more of the questions, you could be in trouble. Self-doubt is a major factor in your makeup, one that is keeping you from producing and living a quality life.

No matter how many times you responded with an "Often" or "Sometimes" to the questions in this quiz, the 10-step plan to conquer self-doubt contained in Chapter 3 can help you. If your level of self-doubt is moderate to high (4 or more), the ten steps can teach you to face and overcome those aspects of life that are crippling you. If your level is low (3 and under), the "C.Q." method can teach you to rid yourself of what little self-doubt remains and give you a great deal of insight about how self-doubt can be combatted in both your life and the lives of those you love.

C.Q. QUIZ

QUESTION	OFTEN	SOMETIMES	NEVER
Do I feel inferior to others?			
Do I think I'm wrong before I consider that someone else might be?			
Do I think others are talking about me?			
Do I worry about whether or not others like me?			
Do I miss out on opportunities because I don't try?			
Do I feel envious of a friend's accomplishments, but am I unwilling to test my own ability for fear I might fail?			
Does another's criticism threaten my feelings of self-confidence and worth?			
Do I avoid getting into new relationships for fear I'll be rejected?			
Do I eat, smoke, or drink alcohol excessively?			
Do I make excuses for myself?			
Do I have trouble accepting compliments?			
Do I question my social skills, my appearance, my wardrobe, and do I compare myself to others?			
Do I overcompensate for my insecurities with boisterous, boastful, forceful, or hostile behavior—or withdrawal?			

THE CONFIDENCE QUOTIENT

At the end of the book, we will ask you these same questions again. If you apply the ten steps that "C.Q." describes to conquer self-doubt in various situations as they arise, you will almost surely see a major difference in the "before" and "after" scores.

People in every segment of society, regardless of their achievements, age, sex, culture, or social class, are hurt by self-doubt. It can overwhelm a man going through a mid-life crisis or a woman unhappy in her profession. It can attack a homemaker who wants more from her daily routine or a teenager struggling for approval and independence.

Today we are faced with endless choices about the future. We have more options in careers, family life, and leisure time than ever before. Men have a new-found freedom to nurture their children and display emotions, while women have more opportunities outside the house. Couples do not feel as much pressure to bear children to make their lives complete. And as we live longer, there is more opportunity for travel and adventure after retirement. Children and teenagers are exposed to a variety of lifestyles and must make difficult decisions about their education and their involvement with alcohol, drugs, and sex.

But such freedoms can create feelings of uncertainty. Today there are few rules or guidelines to follow or role models to emulate. There is no way to gauge if we're doing "the right thing."

With so many different paths to choose from, deciding which one to take can be difficult. Once you make a decision, you wonder if you've made the right one and compare your choice to that of others. "Maybe theirs was a better decision," you tell yourself. And then you worry. "Maybe I won't succeed. Maybe I won't be happy. Maybe I won't impress others as much as I'd like."

If you continually question your decisions or compare yourself to others, it is easy to feel let down when something goes wrong. The slightest mistake can cause your self-image to capsize. The more you dwell on those mistakes, the more quickly you drown in the depths of self-doubt.

If you don't learn to take action and control your feelings of dissatisfaction, you can become locked in a personal prison of self-doubt. Constant negative programming can cause you to look for positive external reinforcements from food, alcohol, drugs, gambling, or extramarital affairs. Or it can paralyze you by causing severe depression, lack of will, or lifelong phobias.

Self-doubt can:

threaten interpersonal relationships;

prevent communication;

destroy marriages;

inhibit sexual performance and;

satisfaction;

hinder children's developmental potential;

create dissatisfaction among homemakers;

cripple executive ability;

suppress creative expression;

lead to alcoholism and drug abuse.

People are often just as afraid to let go of the doubts in their lives as they are to hold on to them. The doubts they harbor keep them safe. They protect them from failing just as they prevent them from succeeding.

Self-doubt is a safety valve people turn on when they want an excuse to avoid making decisions or when they're afraid to take risks for fear of failure. It is a scapegoat that exempts them from taking action.

Not all doubt is bad. When that little voice inside of you warns you not to enter a business deal that might be bad or prevents you from saying something to a friend that you might later regret, you're being cautious. When you suggest that your seventeen-year-old daughter travel to the ski resort on the charter bus with her friends instead of driving the car, your concern is for her safety; you're using sound judgment. The doubt you sense is helping you make good decisions.

But doubt doesn't always work for you. It can hinder your belief in yourself and threaten your ability to make plans. It tells you that you will never be as good as you should be and feeds you bitter helpings of inadequacy. It is the biggest obstacle you will encounter in attaining your goals.

Self-doubt is at the base of such excuses as:

"I can't do it;"

"I don't have the skills;"

"I'm not creative;"

"I'm stuck in a rut and there is no way out;"

"He or she can do it better, so why should I try?"

"Nothing ever goes my way;"

"Why do bad things always happen to me?"

"I'll never overcome this problem;"

"My life will never get better."

Listening to negative self-talk is dangerous because we begin to believe what we've been telling ourselves. When our ego is deflated and we've deserted our dreams, it is easy to become anxious, depressed, irritable, self-conscious, angry, listless, and dissatisfied. And because our minds are not separate from our bodies, physical problems often accompany self-doubt. Headaches, insomnia, colds, flus, ulcers, stomach aches, and muscle pain are common physical complaints of those who listen to the negative messenger.

If we allow self-criticism to chip away at the fountain of self-confidence that keeps positive, constructive energies flowing within us, others will begin to doubt our ability as well. As our self-respect dwindles, we respond to others negatively too. We resent our friends' accomplishments rather than celebrate them.

When we feel unsure of ourselves, we try harder than ever to prove ourselves to family, friends and coworkers. Rather than learn from others, we take exception to their suggestions, directions, and criticisms. We become so concerned about justifying our actions that we are unable to take steps to grow and reach new goals.

Some people try to conceal self-doubt by hiding behind loud, aggressive, selfish, or even hostile behavior. They pretend that they're in control, that they have all the answers, and that they don't need anyone's support. But their actions don't fool others too often, because most of us know that when we feel good about ourselves, we aren't obsessed by the need to prove ourselves to others.

Life is laden with challenges and opportunities. Yet so often people become disappointed when they don't succeed immediately. They use one disappointment or mistake as an excuse not to try again. *To succeed you have to try. To be content, you must first be content with yourself.* You can't consider yourself a victim, meekly letting problems and discouragement overtake you.

No matter how you've handled the doubt in your life, you probably know how overwhelming self-doubt can be. To break out of this self-defeating lifestyle, you have to want to turn the power around. Once you understand your doubting nature, you can utilize your energy to create new alternatives. You can trust yourself and your decisions. You won't need to be envious of other people's successes. You will be able to learn from their achievements and use them as a source of motivation. Building your self-esteem—conquering your self-doubt—is a constant process that involves continual evaluation of where you've been and where you want to be.

Once you learn how to control self-doubt, you will feel better about other people as well as yourself. You will be more willing to take risks outside your "comfort zone." You will exchange feelings of inadequacy for the ability to draw upon resources that will help you find the strength to test new experiences and accomplish your goals. You won't need approval from others because you will realize that the secret to personal satisfaction comes from within.

2

Self-Doubt On The Job

SELF-CONFIDENCE is not something you're born with. It's not a trait that is passed on genetically. Just because your parents are self-assured does not mean that you will live a life free from self-doubt. Neither does it mean that if your parents have little self-confidence that you're destined for a lifetime of low self-esteem.

As with most acquired characteristics, the groundwork for your self-image was laid during the first few years of life. By the time you were four or five, much of the foundation of your self-esteem was set. As you grew, the messages you received from your parents, siblings, relatives, teachers, and other important people in your life had a direct effect on how you felt about yourself. And you will continue to project that same self-image throughout your life unless you discover a need to consciously try to change that picture of yourself.

During the first few months of life when a child is dependent on his parents to fulfill all his needs, an infant begins to interpret his parents' actions and reactions. Although he can't reason or understand, he receives clear messages of love and affection or resentment and anger through touch, sound, and eye contact. If the messages are positive, the infant begins to develop a sense of trust and security. If the messages are negative, the child develops suspicion and apprehension of the world and people in it.

Today, because parents can choose to have their children born in birthing centers where the mother and newborn are not separated after birth, a strong bond—or a sense of trust and security—between mother and infant can begin immediately. And as more fathers take part in their children's births and care for them during the first few months, infants may be more likely to develop a close relationship bond with their fathers as well.

No matter what the circumstances of their birth, most infants have someone to give them attention and fulfill their needs during their first few months of life, whether it was a mother, father, grandparent, or a babysitter, and so were able to develop a certain level of trust in those around them. From my experience, it appears to be premature or sickly babies, who spend months in the hospital with plenty of health care but little nurturing, or children who are put up for adoption and who spend their first few months of life in institutions or multiple foster homes, who often grow up lacking a sense of trust and security.

As an infant develops and begins to do things for himself—lift his head, turn over, crawl, walk, and speak—he realizes that he is a separate being from his parents. He begins to explore the world while continuing to look to his parents for reinforcement and verification.

When parents encourage their child and recognize his achievements, the child forms a positive attitude about himself and develops a sense of both self-worth and independence. And if the parents' love and support does not wane, even when the child does not succeed, that child builds the inner resources he needs to handle failure in a healthy way.

Problems with self-doubt arise when parents continually send negative messages to their child, because eventually the child begins to draw negative conclusions about himself. Parents who are struggling to overcome feelings of insecurity and who are dissatisfied with their lives often cannot provide positive reinforcement to their child and, frequently, have unrealistic expectations of him.

A young child does not yet know how to weigh and evaluate criticism. He believes everything his parents tell him. Eighteen-month-old Stevie colors a tree purple and shows it to his father. Instead of recognizing his son's accomplishment, the father scolds his son for coloring a tree purple. Subconsciously, the father is trying to overcome his own sense of failure by asking the child to be perfect, but even at that young age, Stevie internalizes his father's negative attitude. If his father constantly finds fault with what he does, Stevie will begin to develop doubts about his abilities. The opposite also holds true. If Stevie's father praises his son for a job well done (the color of the tree is insignificant at such a young age), Stevie will have taken one more step toward a healthy ego. Children are eager to please. They want to win their parents' approval so that Mom and Dad will continue to love and care for them.

A child who is constantly chastised for making mistakes or rarely praised for accomplishments can only develop a weak self-image. As an adult, he has a great need for others' approval and has trouble finding satisfying relationships. He develops feelings of worth lessness, inadequacy, and shame. To prove his worth, he may often set unrealistic goals and high, rigid standards. He goes through life looking for approval from others rather than seeking it from within himself. Or he may take the opposite approach and try to prove his worth by overpowering others.

Children whose parents encourage them to succeed and who teach them to learn from their mistakes develop fewer self-doubts and are equipped with the abilities they need to overcome the doubts they do develop.

A parent's job is not easy. Over-praising a child can be unhealthy, too. If Stevie is never corrected, as he grows older he will develop a false sense of self that is vastly different from the world's view of him. If he was always perfect in his parents' eyes, he may think that he is always right, regardless of how many people disagree with him.

PHIL: NEVER GOOD ENOUGH

Phil is a forty-two-year-old land developer who, no matter how much money he made, was never satisfied. He was never pleased with his accomplishments and continually told himself that he could have done more, or could have done it better.*

For years Phil had to fill every minute of the day by doing something constructive. He couldn't go to the beach without reading a book. He couldn't go away for a weekend in the mountains with his wife unless he took his portable computer with him and tackled a new program. He felt good about himself

---

* For more information on defensive character styles, read *Body, Self and Soul* by Rosenberg, Rand and Asay.

only when he was performing because that was the only time his parents had praised him when he was young. Phil's mother and father had simply wanted him to do well, but their good intentions left Phil with feelings of inadequacy if he didn't succeed at everything he attempted.

Phil socialized only with people who would let him assume a take-charge position. He was uncomfortable around people he felt were his intellectual or social equals because they made him doubt his abilities.

To prove his superiority, Phil treated his wife, Judy, more like a child than a partner. After ten years of marriage, Judy was tired of being made to feel inferior and asked Phil to try to change, and to seek help doing it.

Judy's plea was no surprise to Phil. He wanted to change. "I didn't feel good about my life; I was tired of being obsessed with success and tired of wondering if I'd ever be good enough," Phil confesses. "I wanted to learn to accept myself just for me, not for what I could do."

Through therapy, Phil was able to understand why he felt he needed to prove himself to others. "My parents always wanted me to do better," Phil recalls. "Everything I did had to have a purpose. I never remember just being loved for being me. The only self-image I had was related to how much I accomplished."

Phil had to learn a different value system in order to overcome his self-doubts. He had to balance the voice inside him that pushed him to succeed with another voice that told him it was okay to relax and to let others help him take care of himself. For Phil, the change has been slow and arduous, but he says it is worth the effort. And Judy, who is enjoying a less demanding, more loving husband, says it's worth it, too.

"DOUBTING" SONDRA

At age thirty-two, Sondra doubts her ability to choose the right spouse. In the past five years, she has broken two engagements and just left her most recent boyfriend. Tired of flitting from one relationship to another, and wanting to settle down, Sondra sought help.

Sondra describes her father as an old-fashioned man who made all the family's decisions. "My dad felt that because I was a girl I didn't have much worth," she explains. "In his eyes, the best thing I could do was get married so that he could give the family business to my husband."

Looking back, it was easy for Sondra to remember what it was like when she was young. "My parents didn't give me much room to explore and venture out on my own," she says. "My dad worked constantly and my mother was always off to bridge clubs and social functions, leaving me with the house keeper, who did everything for me.

"When the time came for me to go to college, my parents decided that I should enroll in a legal secretary program even though I wanted to attend a four-year business school. It was their money and I had no say."

Through counseling, Sondra has been able to realize that she has the power to make her own decisions. She's beginning to trust herself and her judgment, and she understands that she is going to have to allow herself to make mistakes and still feel good about herself.

As for marriage, the first thing Sondra has decided is that she won't settle for a man who will not recognize her worth as an individual. And she's determined to convince her father of her abilities to take over the family jewelry business. Then, if she marries, her husband can join her in running the business—if he wants to.

OVERCOMING THE PAST

Recognizing patterns in your past that have led to your self-doubts is not any easy process. Some people feel wrong blaming their parents for their problems insisting that they take responsibility for their own actions. Others, whose parents have died, feel guilty accusing them because they are unable to defend themselves. Still others are afraid that looking back will only cause resentment and affect the relationship they have with their parents today.

Most of our parents did the best job they could raising us and helped us develop many good qualities. No parent is capable of providing everything for a child at the right time and to just the right degree because, after all, they too have human frailties that interfere with their good intentions. It is usually with such good intentions that parents are demanding or critical. They don't purposely try to hurt their children or fill them with doubts and fears.

In order to build the part of our self-image that we feel is lacking, we must forgive our parents' imperfections and look ahead at how we can develop necessary traits that will help us to overcome the self-doubt that entered our lives early on.

Many of us seek relationships in our adult lives that are similar to the one we had with our parents when we were a child because we are drawn to what is familiar and comfortable. Even if we did not like the relationship we had with our parents, we surround ourselves with people—spouses, bosses, friends—who act as our parents did or who allow us to act as we did when we were young. Instead of overcoming the self-doubts that began in our childhood, we nourish them and watch them grow.

But how, after twenty, thirty, forty or more years of following certain patterns and harboring self-doubts, can people change? Remember that people change only when they want to. It is not something you can force on anyone or that can be forced on you. Something inside you must say, "I have to do something about this," or, "I just can't handle the pain anymore." The doubt you experience must cause you some type of pain or discomfort for you to take the initiative to find a different way to approach your life and overcome your fears.

Often it is a crisis that will bring about the desire or need for change. It may be an ailment that has made you realize that your body is suffering from the mental pain you're experiencing. Or a life-threatening illness may make you see how pointless it can be to live a life filled with self-doubt. It may be a divorce that propels you to change your mental image or a new love who makes you more aware of your positive traits.

No matter what the motivating force, you can change if you are willing to uncover the origin of your doubts and confront them head on. If you allow yourself to look back, you'll see that the image you have of yourself today and the way you relate to other people is probably directly linked to the way you were treated as a child. While you may not be able to remember how your parents responded to you when you were very young, it's easy to infer if you look at the way they treated you as you grew older and how they act toward you today. The way they react toward you as an adult is probably not much different from the way they've always treated you.

Ask yourself the following questions to help you get an idea of how your past contributed to your feelings of self-doubt versus self-confidence. Circle the phrase *in* each statement that best describes how your parents reacted toward you.

My parents typically:

encouraged/discouraged me to try new things;

showed love all the time/only when I was successful (made the little league team, was selected for choir);

comforted/chastised me when I showed emotion;

helped me/competed against me;

praised me/berated me;

called attention to/seldom mentioned physical shortcomings;

trusted/did not trust me;

were interested/uninterested in my accomplishments.

These statements will help you remember incidents in your past that you may be able to use as you complete the 10-step plan for overcoming self-doubt outlined in Chapter 3.

As children we seldom questioned our parents' evaluation of us. But as adults, we have the ability to reason. We can weigh the opinions our parents had of us and learn to overcome what we consider false assessments.

Too often, as adults, we try to prove ourselves to our parents, even when our parents live miles away or are no longer alive. We continue to try to fulfill their expectations. Or we go to the other extreme and try to get back at them by doing the opposite of what they wanted. Either way we lose, because we've never really given ourselves a chance to discover who we are and what we want.

Our past is a very strong force in our lives. But that force can be redirected. If we allow ourselves to learn from our past, we can use it to guide our future.

3

BE YOUR OWN THERAPIST: A 10-STEP PLAN TO CONQUER SELF-DOUBT

WE are all familiar with the doubting side of our personality. In fact, that negative voice within us is sometimes so loud that we can't hear the other, positive, voice. I've developed a 10-step plan that will enable you to become reacquainted with the confident side of yourself, the part of you that gives the encouragement you need to try and ultimately to succeed.

Learning how to overcome self-doubt does not mean that you will be—or would want to be—doubt free. When used appropriately, doubt is an important, healthy part of your life. It helps you to maintain perspective and to question decisions, judgments, motivations, ideals, and needs. It is when self-doubt runs rampant and is not balanced by self-trust and self-acceptance that you begin to lose faith in your abilities and lack determination to meet goals and attempt new challenges.

As you take part in this process of rediscovering your strength and confidence, you will be using a method that encompasses visualization techniques. This basic mental process goes beyond thinking and allows you to see with your mind's eye.[1] By using this powerful tool for overcoming self-doubt, you will become more aware than ever of how your thoughts and experiences affect your actions. You will have new-found ability to change negative thoughts into positive ones.

The goal of the 10-step plan is to allow you to visualize images of the doubting and reinforcing sides of your personality. At first it may take some time to create those images and to integrate them into your thinking process. But if you continue to use the 10 steps, those images will begin working for you at a deep subconscious level. Your confidence will increase and your doubts will diminish.

To give you an idea of how the 10-step plan can be used

in someone's life, I have included examples of how a woman named Susan responded at each of the steps. You'll see how Susan used the techniques to help conquer the doubts in her life.

The first time you use the plan, you may need an hour or two to complete it. You can go through as many steps as you like at one time or work on one step each day for ten days. Try to complete at least one step each session. If you stop working in the middle of a step, it will be difficult to recapture your thoughts when you return.

Before you begin working with the 10 steps, let your family or friends know that you will need some time to yourself. Plan ahead so that you can be alone in the house, or take some time when family members or roommates are busy. Wait until the children are napping, playing at a neighbor's, or until your spouse can keep them occupied. You may even want to take the phone off the hook or let your family or friends know that you don't want to receive any calls.

You'll reap more benefits from the exercise if you can work with it in a quiet place where you can be by yourself. Take along a pencil to write down your responses to each of the ten steps, either in the space provided in this book or on a pad of paper. Settle comfortably into a couch or lean back in a comfortable reclining chair.

Take a few deep breaths and try to clear your mind of the day's activities and problems so that you can concentrate on the exercise. The next few minutes are just for you!

STEP 1: IDENTIFY YOUR DOUBTS

WHAT'S BOTHERING YOU?

As you relax, close your eyes and think of the area in your life about which you are feeling the most concern or fear at this moment. Try to identify the most pressing self-doubt you are currently experiencing. What in your life makes you feel uncertain or anxious? In other words, what's really troubling you and, more importantly, why?

Identifying self-doubt is an important part of the process of overcoming it because we often don't take time to sort out our feelings. We let one bad feeling pile on top of another until the core of our concern becomes buried or muddled. Before you can learn how to control feelings of inadequacy or inability, you must be able to understand how it is affecting your life. Putting thoughts into words is another way to help you pinpoint your doubt.

Begin by asking and answering the following questions:

> Why do I feel anxious or afraid? What one overpowering issue is constantly on my mind?
>
> What is standing in the way of the future I want for myself?

With those answers in mind, write down your present self-doubt:

That I will not be able to handle both jobs. That the promotion will be taken away from me. That I will never find a suitable partner.

If you can't put your doubt into words, read these brief examples of self-doubt and the longer description of Susan's self-doubt. Once you've read about Susan's doubt, come back and try to put your concerns into words.

Examples of self-doubt:

> I'm bored with my daily routine; I'll never get out of this rut;

I'm afraid I don't satisfy my partner;

I want to make a change, but I don't think my family understands my needs;

I feel trapped in an unhappy marriage and can't see any way out;

I left the working world to have children;

I'll never be able to find a good job again;

I worry no one will need me now that my children are grown;

I don't have the skills to find a job I really want;

I'll never get out of this dead-end job;

I don't think I'll ever really succeed.

SUSAN'S SELF-DOUBT: "As a wife, mother and working woman, I am being stretched in all directions. I want to develop my career, but whenever I take steps toward business goals, I feel as if I'm turning my back on my two children and my responsibility as a mother. I doubt if I'll ever be able to fulfill my career goals."

FULLY DESCRIBE YOUR SELF-DOUBT

Once you've identified your self-doubt, embellish the description. Pretend that you're telling a friend how the doubt or fear affects your life. Don't be afraid to talk out loud in answering these questions:

How does the doubt make me feel?

What types of problems does it pose in my life?

Why is this doubt part of my life?

How long have I felt this way?

Describe your self-doubt using the questions above as guidelines:

_____

_____

_____

_____

_____

_____

SUSAN DESCRIBES HER DOUBT: "Steve and I feel that we have adapted well to being a two-career family. We share the housework, spend time helping the boys with their homework, and take turns chauffeuring them to soccer and Cub Scouts. Six years ago, I opened a gift boutique with a few thousand dollars and a lot of ingenuity and determination, while Steve continued to work for a large retail chain. After months of hard work, the business grew and Steve quit his job to help me expand the business. Today, the boutique provides the sole source of income for our family.

"Even though Steve and I are proud of my foresight and the store's success, we still regard the financial solvency of our family as Steve's ultimate responsibility and the domestic tasks as mine. I can create a dynamite advertising campaign, but if the dinner isn't on the table at six o'clock, I feel guilty. I worry that I'm depriving my family of an all-American homelife.

"The trouble is that I'm a product of the 'Father Knows Best' and 'Donna Reed Show' generation. The women on those television programs were my role models as was my own mother, who was perfectly content with being a homemaker, and did an incredible job.

"Steve and I made a decision to raise a family. I feel that the boys have to be my first priority at all times. I tell myself that I won't get to focus on my career until Ted and Gary are in their teens and that's seven years away.

"I don't think I can have my idea of a successful career and family at the same time because to me success means being the best. When I'm at work, I tell myself I'm not being a good mother and think of all the things I'm not doing at home. When I'm with the boys and I get an idea for the business, I tell myself I should be devoting more time to work."

STEP 2: THINK BACK TO WHEN YOUR DOUBT BEGAN

Our reactions to events in our lives are usually based on how we handled experiences in the past. This step will help you to understand how and when your current self-doubt began.

With your eyes closed, try to recall how the doubt you are experiencing first began. When was the seedling of doubt, which grew unnoticed until it overpowered your positive thoughts, planted?

Think back to a time when you were a young child. Try to remember an early experience when you felt the same anxious feeling that your present doubt is creating in your life. Push your memory back as far as it can go. Try to remember an incident in grade school or even kindergarten. The earlier you can recall feeling the type of self-doubt you are feeling now, the better.

Ask yourself the following questions to prompt your memory:

How did I feel when I was overcome by the doubt?

What event, action, or comment caused the doubt to surface?

How did I deal with uncertainty in my life?

How did my mother contribute to my feelings of inadequacy?

How did my father add to my feelings of doubt?

How did my sisters, brothers, aunts, uncles, cousins, friends, teachers, clergymen, or coaches affect my self-esteem?

Don't worry if it takes you a while to remember details in your past or to recall a specific incident. It's often difficult to think of frustrating times because we tend to push them aside and replace them with good memories. Just relax and be patient. Let your thoughts flow.

If you need a little help to get through this step, take a few minutes to look at an old photo album that includes pictures of you as a child. Look at the photos and try to recall the circumstances. Does anything in the photo—your Easter dress, your dog, Charlie, or your father's square chin—help you to remember what used to make you feel inadequate, uncertain, unworthy or less confident than you would have liked?

Another good way to summon old feelings is to rummage through school papers or scrapbooks. Maybe you'll find the second grade report card you were too embarrassed to bring home. Or you may come across the red ribbon you won at the elementary school track meet, only to have someone tease you because it wasn't a first-place blue ribbon.

Looking through memorabilia can be a great time machine that sends your mind spinning back to incidents you've tucked away. You need to remember those experiences of yesterday if you want to be able to control self-doubt tomorrow.

Describe an event or several events in your past when you felt doubtful, fearful, cautious, or anxious about your ability or performance, or a reaction or decision:

_____

_____

_____

_____

THE CONFIDENCE QUOTIENT

_____

_____

_____

By comparing an early doubting experience to the way you are feeling today, you will more easily be able to learn how to overcome self-doubt.

SUSAN RECALLS PAST EXPERIENCES: "I really think my doubt about my ability to succeed in the business world began when I was about twelve. I used to read in the newspaper classified ads and became frustrated by the lack of job opportunities for girls.

"It infuriated me that almost the only job available to girls my age was babysitting. In the 1960s, boys had so many options not available to girls. They could be paperboys, bagboys, busboys, or start a lawn mowing service.

"I wanted to prove myself in business and show others that it wasn't just 'a man's world.' When I was eighteen, I seriously considered joining the army to become a nurse. I dreamed of working at Walter Reed Army Hospital in Maryland. But I let a friend's silly comment sway my decision.

"'You'll never get a boyfriend if you're too smart,' my friend teased. 'Remember, boys don't make passes at girls who wear glasses!'

"I wore glasses, so that awful saying stuck in my mind. I began to believe that if I went to college I would never get married. I thought the magic answer to becoming a successful woman was to cook, sew, and clean. I had a perfect example to follow—a mother who did everything around the house and was content doing it. Not only did she clean and cook, she manicured the yard, rewired worn out lamps, and even knew how to fix a leaky faucet.

"I also remember my father desperately wanting me to do well in school. He wanted the best from me. He used to say he didn't have 'average' daughters, meaning that he wouldn't accept a report card with any grade below a B. When I didn't meet his standards, I felt as if I had let him down."

STEP 3: PICTURE YOUR DOUBTING SIDE

SEE WHAT YOUR DOUBTER LOOKS LIKE

Now that you have identified the way in which your current self-doubt(s) began, you're ready to see what the doubting side of you looks like.

In this step, you will use visualization techniques to develop a mental image of that part inside of you that causes you to doubt—what I call "the doubter." Your brain is used to thinking with images and you'll find that by creating a mental picture of your doubter, it will be easier to overcome your doubts.

Make believe that your doubter has size, shape, and form. It can be a person, animal, color, sound, or any image you create. There are no rules to follow. It is perfectly acceptable for a woman to picture a male doubter or a man to imagine a female one.

Concentrate and make a mental picture of the doubter inside you. This step can take a few minutes. Don't rush yourself. Give yourself time to be inventive.

Describe what your doubter looks like:

_____
_____
_____
_____
_____
_____

Now, take a moment to draw your doubter in the space provided below or on your pad of paper. Your artistic skills don't have to be well developed for you to make a simple sketch that will give you a workable image of your doubter.

Don't worry if the mental image of your doubter is not perfectly clear or if your drawing does not seem imaginative. Whatever you think of or sketch will work. You can always change it later.

SUSAN DRAWS HER DOUBTER: "I drew a picture of the storybook character Tinkerbell, held prisoner in the glass jar placed over her by Captain Hook. My doubter keeps me in the trap. The sides of the glass jar represent all of my responsibilities. Outside of the jar I see a whole world waiting to be explored, but I'm bound inside. I have wings and I'm ready to fly, but I can't get out."

To help you identify your doubter, here are examples of doubters other people have described:

A mother	A warrior
A father	A little girl
A baby in a womb	A monkey
A devil	The color black
A little boy	The screeching sound of automobile brakes
A prisoner with a ball and chain	

GIVE YOUR DOUBTER A NAME

Once your doubter has taken on a form, both through the image you've put on paper and the one you can clearly see in your mind, give your doubter a name. Decide what you will call it based on its size, appearance, behavior, or how it makes you feel.

Name your doubter:

_____

Other examples of names for doubters are listed below:

Mother	The Devil
Father	Slouch
Little Girl	Skinny Plain Jane
Little Boy	Fatso
The Apologizer	The Villain
The Wolf	

SUSAN NAMES HER DOUBTER: "I named my doubter 'Trapped Tinkerbell.'"

STEP 4: THANK YOUR DOUBTER

This is the most difficult step in the plan to understand, but when you complete the entire formula, you will realize its importance.

You now have a mental picture of your doubter and have given it a name. Take a moment to thank your doubter. Yes, I said thank it. Your doubter has worked very hard for you throughout your life.

It may be hard to believe, but your doubter does not just hinder you. Ask yourself how your doubting, scrutinizing, and judging side has helped you.

Has your doubter protected you and kept you safe by not letting you cross the street when a car is approaching? By questioning bad business deals? Has your doubter given you motivation and drive by planting feelings of guilt if you're not productive? By only accepting top quality work? Has your doubter kept you in good company or made you feel proud by scrutinizing your friends and questioning relationships? By evaluating your actions? Describe what the doubter or judge within you has done to help you during your life:

_____

_____

_____

_____

_____

HOW SUSAN'S DOUBTER HAS HELPED HER: "By doubting my ability to be able to balance my career and homelife, 'Trapped Tinkerbell' has kept me from getting headstrong and selfish. She has kept me from pursuing some of my business goals and has made me spend time at home. In doing so, she has helped me enjoy some very special times with my two children. She has taught me that not all my feelings of worth have to come from the business side of my life. There are things I do each day for my family of which I can feel proud.

"By always judging my actions, my doubter has also kept me working hard at home and at the boutique. I'm willing to accept only top-quality work from myself, whether I'm baking a pie or redecorating the store. Because of that, I'm always striving to achieve."

STEP 5: DO YOU REALLY WANT TO CHANGE?

This is a very crucial part of the entire 10-step process for overcoming self-doubt. At this point, you must decide if the way your doubter has been working in your life is acceptable to you.

Or, would you prefer to change some of the ways your doubter reacts? For example, maybe you want to be productive, but are tired of always being driven by fear. Then, yes, you want to make changes in your doubter.

If, on the other hand, you are happy with the way your doubter has been working in your life or feel you cannot make a change at this time, do not proceed with the remaining steps of the formula. If you try to change when you are not really ready to, your doubter may fill you with new worries, excuses, or anxieties that will sabotage your attempts to change.

There are times when we need to let the doubter have a prominent role in our lives for a while. One client I treated felt this way. She was a divorced woman whose self-doubt centered around getting involved with men. Her doubter put up roadblocks when situations arose in which she began to become emotionally involved. The woman wanted to allow her creative side to help her show her feelings and accept affection, but when asked if she was willing to change she said, "No."

Her doubter was giving her the protection she needed at that particular time in her life. Her teenage son was in the hospital being treated for drug addiction. Her doubter was helping her to cope with the situation by keeping her emotions suppressed. It was her way of dealing with her son's problems. She was not ready to share how she was feeling with a male companion and so was not ready for a romantic relationship.

Although she did not proceed with the remaining steps at that time, she knew that, when the issue with her son was resolved and she was ready to meet a man, she could go back to the ten steps and discover her creative side, just as you will discover if you are ready to proceed with step 6.

Write down your decision. Do you want to change the way your doubter is affecting your life? If so, why?

_____

_____

_____

SUSAN'S DECISION: "Now that I understand that my doubter has helped me at times, I see that she's not all bad. But I feel that my doubter plays too big a part in my life. I'm ready and willing to change. I want to get rid of that trapped feeling and allow myself to take risks. I don't want to be afraid of failing. I don't want to surround myself with unwarranted fears that if I strive in my career I will hurt my family. I'd like a balance in my life, something I can't have with Tinkerbell shackled in that glass prison."

STEP 6: PICTURE YOUR CREATIVE SIDE

Before you move on, remember that your doubter— the one you've named—must be willing to accept any alterations you consider for your life. Only if you can convince your doubter of the benefits of the changes you are considering will it let you feel satisfied with your decisions. And only then will you begin to make positive change.

DESCRIBE THE REINFORCER WITHIN YOU

Now use your imagination to develop a picture of the positive side of yourself. This time, look for the creative, helpful, resourceful side. This is the reinforcer within you that gives you a sense that "Yes, I can," rather than "No, I can't." Your reinforcer lets you take risks and helps you try new things.

After you've made contact with your reinforcing side, decide what it looks like. Give it a concrete form. Just as when you were describing your doubter, let your mind run free as you develop your reinforcer. It, too, can be a person of either sex, an animal, a color, a sound, or anything else.

As you try to describe your reinforcing side, ask yourself:

How does my reinforcer make me feel?

What can it do for me in the future?

Write down a few of the characteristics you associate with the positive, creative side of you. How does the reinforcer within you look, act, feel and react?

___

___

___

___

___

___

___

___

SUSAN'S REINFORCER: "I see my creative side as a part of me that is willing to take chances. It does not want me just to exist, but to experience all I can without detriment to my family. It reminds me of 'Auntie Mame' in the Broadway musical. My reinforcer, like Auntie Mame, is not vulnerable and mousy but a little tough, a little daring. She's not trapped by life's circumstances as Tinkerbell is.

"Auntie Mame in the play was always ready for the next adventure. She felt life was a banquet and that most people were starving to death!

"I want my reinforcer to be more like Auntie Mame. I don't want to make excuses for not trying. I want to meet new challenges. I want to believe in myself and my family's willingness to support me.

"In fact, maybe my adventures and success wil add excitement to my family's life. Maybe my boys will benefit by my being a new role model for them to judge the women that will come into their lives. Maybe then they will know that a woman can have the best of both worlds."

Just as you did with your doubter, sketch a picture of the reinforcing side of you:

GIVE YOUR REINFORCER A NAME

Now that you have a picture of your reinforcer, give it a name as you did with your doubter.

Name your reinforcer: _____

SUSAN NAMES HER REINFORCER: "I named my reinforcer 'Auntie Mame' so that when I call on it I'll be reminded of that confident, vibrant woman."

Names that people have given their reinforcers are listed below:

Painter	Woman on a Powerful Horse
Dancer	Princess
Agile Athlete	Angel
Goddess Diana	Well-Proportioned Woman
Racer	Blue
Butterfly	

STEP 7: CHANGE NEGATIVE MESSAGES TO POSITIVE ONES

Your reinforcer has power to do almost anything as long as your doubter accepts the changes. Reassure your doubter that you have not forgotten it, but that you are working to make your life better. Your reinforcer is going to come up with two or three new alternatives for ways in which you can approach areas in your life about which you have doubts. Take a few minutes to think about how your doubter has handled specific situations in the past.

Ask yourself:

What has my doubter been saying to me?

How has my doubter made me feel?

How have I reacted to those feelings?

Write down any feelings you have about how your doubter has reacted to situations in the past:

_____

_____

THE CONFIDENCE QUOTIENT

_____

_____

_____

_____

_____

_____

_____

Now, with your eyes closed, let your creative, positive side take over. Think of new ways your reinforcer can help you react to old frustrations and new challenges.

Decide how your reinforcer can change the negative messages your doubter feeds you into positive ones. For example, if your doubter second guesses your decisions, your reinforcer can encourage you to trust your judgment and intuition. Your reinforcer can assure you that you have looked at all sides of the issue and that you are doing what you believe is best.

Your reinforcer can give you permission to fail. It can remind you that none of us are right all the time and that everyone makes mistakes. Or, it can let you know that you can't expect to do something perfectly the first time you try.

Remember, your reinforcer cannot do anything without your doubter's permission. You must give your doubter a certain amount of power. That way, it will be willing to work with you to find new ways of approaching areas of your life that have caused you discomfort in the past.

In the space below, list new approaches that you can use to confront specific problem areas in your life:

_____

_____

_____

_____

_____

_____

_____

_____

Once you've made this "shopping list," promise yourself that you will try these new approaches to old problems.

Ask your reinforcer to find new ways to approach doubts about:

success;

what others think about you;

trying new things;

your weight;

your age;

finding a new job;

changing careers; and getting involved with others.

List several of your doubts and ways your newly found reinforcing side can confront them differently than you have in the past:

DOUBT: _____

NEW APPROACH: _____

_____

_____

_____

DOUBT: _____

NEW APPROACH: _____

_____

_____

_____

DOUBT: _____

NEW APPROACH: _____

_____

_____

_____

SUSAN LETS HER CREATIVE SIDE WORK

DOUBT: "I have a terrible fear of failure. I often don't take steps to gain new business knowledge because I'm afraid of how others will react if I don't succeed."

NEW APPROACH: "Auntie Mame is going to tell me that it's okay if I fail as long as I try. She will reinforce the fact that I don't have to prove myself to others."

DOUBT: "I wonder what will happen to the boys if I spend more time at the boutique. What if they get into trouble? What if I'm not there every day when they come home from school? I'll blame myself if something happens to one of them that could have been avoided had I been home."

NEW APPROACH: "My creative side helps me to have more faith in my role as a mother. It tells me that I am doing a good job. Auntie Mame reassures me that I am not forsaking my role at home just because I also choose to become more involved in my career. She tells me that I have the skill to do both well."

DOUBT: "It may sound funny, but sometimes I think I'm more afraid of success than I am of failure. What if my sales campaigns and marketing approaches really blossom? Will Steve feel that I'm trying to overshadow him? Once I start something big, I'm going to have to finish it. Will I be able to follow through?"

NEW APPROACH: "Auntie Mame will tell me that way of thinking is absurd. As my reinforcer, she will help me not to flaunt success. Auntie Mame will remind me that Steve and I are in business together; we're business partners. Whatever we do—individually or together—to foster the business benefits the entire family. At the same time, Auntie Mame will remind me that I can take credit for my personal business achievements without becoming a threat to Steve, and that Steve should be able to succeed in his endeavors without threatening my self-esteem"

"Auntie Mame will let me trust myself to finish what I've started. She'll give me a pep talk if I begin to falter. She will tell me 'Yes, you can!'"

STEP 8: LET YOUR REINFORCER EDIT THE PAST

YOUR REINFORCER COULD HAVE HELPED YOU THEN

You have two or three new tools your reinforcer can use when self-doubt begins to dominate your thoughts. Think back again to the early self-doubt you recreated in step 2. Apply your creative side to that experience and ask yourself:

THE CONFIDENCE QUOTIENT

How could my reinforcer have handled the situation?

How could I have used my new tools to overcome self-doubt in that experience?

What messages could my reinforcer—my positive side—have given me when self doubt began to take over?

How could I have interpreted messages from others differently if the creative side and the doubting side of me had worked in harmony?

Put your feelings on paper:

_____

_____

_____

_____

_____

_____

_____

_____

_____

For example, could you have:

given yourself more confidence in your ability to earn good grades or make the football team or cheerleading squad?

told yourself it was okay if your saddle shoes were not as pretty as your friend's patent leather ones?

given yourself permission to feel bad when you got caught in a white lie, and used the experience to determine how to avoid lying in the future?

told yourself that mistakes were something to learn from when you didn't get the part in the Christmas pageant because you didn't study your lines?

SUSAN LETS HER REINFORCER EDIT THE PAST: "If Auntie Mame had been around when I was frustrated by the lack of money-paying jobs available to girls, she would have given me the courage to be a maverick and question established 'rules.' Someone had to be the first bag girl or busgirl. Auntie Mame would have said, 'Why not you?'

"Instead of choosing not to go to college for fear that I then would never marry, Auntie Mame would have said, 'Nonsense! You can do both.' She would have encouraged me to be myself and stop comparing myself to others.

"When my father got upset that I earned a C in science, even though all my other grades were A's and B's, Auntie Mame would have encouraged me to try harder in that particular area but would have also reminded me of my many above-average talents. She would have helped me see the positive side of myself more often."

How Past Doubts Affect You Today

Now that you've recreated one or two early incidents of self-doubt and have seen how your creative side could have worked to overcome them, you will be able to see how past feelings of doubt tie in with present ones. Ask yourself:

Am I seeking approval today for something bad I did when I was young?

Am I trying to make up for the past?

Did something embarrassing or frightening happen when I was a child that makes me fearful of doing certain things now?

Was I once forced to do something I didn't want to, and do certain experiences now remind me of that?

Write down how your past feelings of doubt relate to your present feelings. What are the similarities?

_____

_____

_____

_____

_____

_____

_____

_____

SIMILARITIES BETWEEN SUSAN'S PAST AND PRESENT DOUBTS: "When I was young I was frustrated by the lack of money-making ventures open to young girls. Similarly, today I become impatient when my role at home holds me back from using my business skills. I tell myself that I'll never get ahead unless I work full time. That's very much like the conclusion I came to in high school when I decided that women who went to college would wind up spinsters. I saw my life as an either/or proposition. As a teen I doubted that I would be able both to get an education and find someone who would love and marry me. Now I doubt that I can be a good mother and a successful businesswoman at the same time.

"My father's desire for above-average grades on report cards made me think I wouldn't please him if I was anything less than excellent. Today, I'm not content with day-to-day accomplishments but always push for superior achievement."

STEP 9: USE YOUR NEW CREATIVE STRATEGY TO CONQUER DOUBT

Use your newfound creative side to control the doubt presently in your life, as you described it in step 1. How can you employ the new tools you have designed to control self-doubt?

Ask your positive side, the reinforcer, to plan a strategy that will help you conquer self-doubt and discover new and uplifting feelings. Recognize and acknowledge that the reinforcer in you has an unlimited arsenal for defense. Your doubter can continue to protect and keep you safe, but only in proportion to how protected and safe you truly want to be. From this moment on, your reinforcer is able to take charge in situations in which you feel overwhelmed by doubt.

What is your new strategy?

_____

_____

_____

_____

_____

_____

_____

_____

SUSAN'S DOUBTER AND REINFORCER WORK TOGETHER: "My doubter is always worrying about living up to somebody else's standards. It never thinks that what I do is enough.

This fear of failure is the glass cage that surrounds me. It traps me. At the same time, Tinkerbell struggles to get out. I'm never at peace with my decisions or actions.

"I'm going to let Auntie Mame free me from the jar that has kept me surrounded by doubt. Auntie Mame will see the positive side of what I'm doing. She will congratulate me for steps I'm taking to forward my career goals and point to past accomplishments.

"Auntie Mame doesn't doubt my accomplishments. She pats me on the back and says, 'Good job!' She gives me credit for what I've done and lets me succeed at my own pace. I don't have to be the high powered executive or the supermom. I can be proud of what I do as Susan. I don't have to prove myself.

"My reinforcer will help to remind me of the good things I have done. Since my father emphasized gettting good grades and rewarded me when I did, I need to set up ways to grade and reward myself— especially since I'm self-employed. I don't get a quarterly review from a boss, so my reinforcer will review my work. When I feel as if I haven't done enough, my reinforcer will help me to make a list of my accomplishments—even if they're as small as delivering ad copy to the newspaper or driving the boys to soccer practice.

"Auntie Mame will help me think of ways to reward my hard work. I've always wanted to learn Spanish and would love to join the tennis club in our neighborhood. By taking those steps, I'll be able to see the benefits of my hard work—it will be like earning an A on a report card or getting a pay raise.

"My reinforcer will show me how to reward myself instead of waiting for someone else to pat me on the back."

STEP 10: CREATE THE FUTURE YOU WANT

Now that you know how to draw upon the creative side of yourself, your doubter should have less influence on your life. When the doubter in you begins to send you negative messages and tries to smother your confidence, call upon your reinforcer and ask for help.

This does not mean that you suddenly will exude self-confidence and never question yourself again. Remember, your doubter has helped you to question circumstances, made you cautious, kept you humble, pushed you to achieve, and forced you to consider other people's feelings. But at times, you've given your doubter too much freedom and control over your life.

Your doubter and reinforcer should work in tandem. They will provide balance in your life. With your reinforcer at work, you no longer have to be threatened by the fear of failure. And since your doubter is always at your disposal, you don't have to worry about taking too big a risk.

When doubt begins to overtake you—when you feel dissatisfied, worthless, anxious, depressed, or lonely—use the 10-step method and use your reinforcer to help overcome self-doubt. Here's a review of the 10 steps to help you in the process of overcoming self-doubt:

STEP 1
IDENTIFY YOUR SELF-DOUBT

What has been bothering you?

Describe your self-doubt.

STEP 2
THINK BACK TO WHEN YOUR DOUBTS BEGAN

Determine when your doubt was planted.

Recreate an early experience of self-doubt.

STEP 3
PICTURE YOUR DOUBTING SIDE

Create a mental image for your "doubter" and give it a name.

STEP 4
THANK YOUR DOUBTER

Your doubter has helped you. Describe how.

STEP 5
DO YOU REALLY WANT TO CHANGE?

You must be ready to have your doubter play a less significant part in your life or your doubter may find excuses for you not to change.

STEP 6
PICTURE YOUR CREATIVE SIDE

Develop an image for your "reinforcer" and give it a name.

STEP 7
CHANGE NEGATIVE MESSAGES TO POSITIVE ONES

Think of two or three "gifts" or positive messages that your reinforcer can give you when doubt begins to surface.

STEP 8
LET YOUR REINFORCER EDIT THE PAST

Determine how your reinforcer could have handled situations in the past when you were troubled by self-doubt, how it could have worked with—not against—your doubter.

STEP 9
USE YOUR CREATIVE STRATEGY TO CONQUER DOUBT

Let your reinforcer work on your present doubts.

STEP 10
CREATE THE FUTURE YOU WANT

Put your reinforcer to work whenever your doubter begins to overshadow you. Now that you are aware of the effect your doubter has had on your life, you can use your reinforcer to balance your doubter and create new alternatives and experiences. You have the resources to live your life the way you want it to be!

4

HOUSEWIFE SYNDROME

IF you're a homemaker who feels depressed, listless, anxious, discouraged, angry, or filled with self-doubt, you're not alone.

You're not the only housewife who feels like boycotting the breakfast dishes, snapping the mop in two, or setting the washing machine on an eternal spin cycle. It is not uncommon to toss and turn when you try to fall asleep at night or to wish in the morning that the family and house could run themselves so that you could escape another day of the same routine. There are plenty of other women like you who are overcome by guilt because they have wonderful children and a loving husband, yet still feel unfulfilled.

Tens of thousands of women in this country suffer from a real and serious malaise, which, until recently, has been ignored or misunderstood. The condition is called neurasthenia [2] and is popularly known as housewife syndrome—or put more simply, chronic self-doubt. It is a feeling of helplessness, of being left out of the world, of feeling small and childlike.

Housewife syndrome attacks both women who worked until their children were born as well as women who have always been full-time homemakers and mothers. Symptoms can strike women of any age or income level.

Housewife syndrome affects women in different ways. Some go for weeks at a time without a sign of self-doubt and then become severely depressed for days without knowing why. Others are constantly burdened with feelings of inadequacy and frustration.

The American housewife feels she must justify her role to a society focused on personal achievement and independence. Not only does she try to prove her worth to her husband and family but to her career minded friends. The harder she tries to justify her role, the more entrenched she becomes in a life where her measuring stick becomes how much she can do for others. She feels trapped in a routine of cleaning, cooking, laundering, and carpools. The more she does for others, the less time she has for personal growth and privacy. And as her family and household demand control her time and energy, her self-esteem begins to fade.

A housewife often feels at the financial mercy of her spouse. While her husband may tell her, and intellectually she knows, that it's "their" money, she feels that she must ask permission before she buys something for herself. And when she does spend money on herself, she often feels guilty. Still other women spend money out of spite. They overspend as a way of dis-playing their anger and making themselves feel powerful.

Asking for permission, refereeing sibling fights, endless vacuuming and dirty pots and pans—that probably isn't any woman's idea of how she should spend her adult life. Most women who want a family have unrealistic expectations of the demands children will make on their lives. After all the excitement and baby showers, the woman is left holding the dirty diapers. And even if she completes each job with speed and agility, and enjoys her domestic role, a woman at home gets little "stroking" for what she does.

One reason housewives are so vulnerable to self-doubt is that they often do not get enough attention from their family. A homemaker's daily routine seems secondary to her husband's career and her children's development. And when life seems monotonous and goals insignificant, it's easy for the paralyzing effects of housewife syndrome to set in.

WHAT NEURASTHENIA IS

Neurasthenia (Latin for nerve weakness) was identified at the turn of the century. At first, physicians believed it occurred in patients whose internal conflict and overwork was placing great stress on their nerve cells. It was seen as a fatigue syndrome, and rest and relaxation was recommended as the best treatment. But this was rarely successful because people who suffered neurasthenia did not usually show signs of overwork.[3] Neurasthenia is now considered the result of psychological, not physical, fatigue, and is described by the American Psychiatric Association as "characterized by...an inability to cope with one's lifestyle."

The women I treat for housewife syndrome, and those across the country who wrote to me after reading interviews with me about the topic in the *Los Angeles Herald-Examiner, The Star,* and *Lady's Circle*, and watching me discuss it on the "John Davidson Show," "Hour Magazine," and the "Phil Donahue" show, have a long list of complaints. They lack energy, ambition, and don't want to get up in the morning. And they are frequently sick with headaches, cold, or flu, which gives them good reason for staying in bed and elicits attention from their families. But it is the feeling of uncontrollable depression and anxiety that usually prompts women to seek help. They feel that their lives lack purpose and that they themselves lack identity.

Neurasthenia primarily affects women who have been brought up to believe that the key to a complete life lies in finding a man and raising a family. Even in our enlightened age, many women never really question their expectations about marriage or becoming a parent. They want a man who will make them feel beautiful, sexy, and loved, and children who will make them feel needed and important and who also will live out their unfulfilled dreams. When their family doesn't live up to their expectations or they discover that it isn't enough to make them happy, they become overcome with self-doubt.

They tell themselves that they're selfish, unable to be satisfied, and too demanding, or they reinforce negative messages. "I can't do anything else." "I don't have any skills." "There must be something wrong with me." "I have everything I thought would make me happy, and I'm miserable." Women who surround themselves with selfdoubt often suffer serious depression and anxiety. Some women, overwhelmed with self-doubt, become afraid to go out of the house and are paralyzed with the household plague known as agoraphobia (an abnormal fear of open spaces and crowds). The more she secludes herself from others, the larger her doubts about her place in the world become. And all the time she's suffering, she builds up resentment with statements like, "Look what I gave up for my husband and the kids!"

Other women who are dissatisfied try to overcome their frustrations by eating, and put on extra pounds. Others fill voids in their lives with shopping sprees. But the chocolate sundaes and silk blouses give only temporary relief, like an aspirin that masks the real cause of a tension headache. A woman will never feel good about herself if she continually looks to others to bring her happiness. She needs not only to feel good about her accomplishments and her family, but about who she is as an individual.

PAMELA: SEDUCED BY THE "AMERICAN DREAM"

Pamela is an attractive thirty-five-year-old brunette. She is a wife and mother of two children, ages three and seven.

When Pamela learned she was pregnant at age twenty-eight, she was ecstatic. She quit her job as a secretary for a real estate firm and looked forward to spending time with her first child.

"I enjoyed being a homemaker until my son was about three," recalls Pamela. "Then I started to get bored and began thinking about looking for work outside the home. I attended an assertiveness training class, and just about the time I was ready to begin job hunting, I became pregnant again. I resigned myself to motherhood and felt fine until my daughter was one year old. Then the tiredness, crankiness, colds, and flus began. I was grumpy and irritable and snapped at the children. I constantly felt 'down,' regardless of my husband's attempts to cheer me up.

"I was sick of making all the meals and keeping the house in tip-top shape," Pamela admits. "I was tired of driving kids to football practice and dancing lessons. And I didn't like being on call if my husband wanted to bring home a business associate for dinner, or having no one to help me with the kids when he had to go out of town for a few days at a time.

"But no one understood how I felt—not even me! I was brought up to believe in the American dream. I was taught that college and career were secondary to finding a man and having babies. But what did that leave me with? How could I feel good about myself when I was always waiting on everyone else without even a paycheck or time off to look forward to?

"I felt guilty that I could feel so miserable when I have such a wonderful husband," Pamela continues. "He brought home good money, didn't hang out at bars, and was a faithful, caring man. But I felt like a parasite—like I depended on him for everything— both good and bad alike."

Pamela used the 10-step plan to help her identify her self-doubts and to begin to overcome them. She realized that she had two main doubts: a fear of inadequacy and a fear of change.

"I doubted that I'd ever be able to feel independent again and I worried that if I did find a job or an interesting pastime, my family would fall apart," Pamela explains. "When I think back to when I was about eight years old, I can remember telling my parents that I wanted to grow up to be someone important. They immediately told me that girls couldn't be important—that they needed someone to take care of them. They said that if my ideas were too big, I'd scare men away."

Pamela saw her doubter as a little girl with her thumb in her mouth—someone who kept her safe and secure. And when she was feeling tired and sick, her husband took care of her—just the way her doubter liked it.

The reinforcer Pamela imagined was a dancer, who was free to come up with new steps and routines and was filled with energy and the will to change. Once Pamela realized that her reinforcer could have just as much control as her doubter, she began to make changes in her life.

Pamela's reinforcer has helped her to get out of her rut. She joined a babysitting co-op so that she had one free day a week to herself. Instead of giving the children a weekly allowance, she let them earn one by doing chores around the house. And she swapped chores with her husband. He cooked two meals a week and she balanced the checkbook. He vacuumed the house once a week and she took the car to the garage to get the tires balanced.

The changes Pamela implemented were small at first, but she had come to an important realization: she did have choices. She could change as little or as much as she wanted or needed.

Once Pamela began to make time for herself, she began taking tennis lessons and joined the auxiliary at the museum of art. With time to pursue her own interests, she felt more relaxed and self-assured and rarely got sick. Pamela decided that she didn't want to return to work—at least not for a few years—but she understood that time away from household responsibilities and family demands gave her the reprieve she needed and deserved.

CREATING ALTERNATIVES IN DAILY ROUTINE

Like Pamela, many women would like to find ways to overcome self-doubt without having to return to the work force. They want to find ways to enjoy their roles as a homemaker.

When a homemaker decides to send the kids to a babysitter so that she can spend the day at the beach, alone, she and others often consider her behavior selfish. Yet a working woman who attends an exercise class after work isn't thought of as being selfish, nor is a man who goes to a baseball game after work.

In A *Circle of Quiet,* author Madeleine L'Engle writes:

> Every so often I need OUT; something will throw me into total disproportion, and I have to get away from everybody—away from all these people I love most in the world—in order to regain a sense of proportion. Often I need to get away completely, if only for a few minutes. My special place is a small brook in a green glade, a circle of quiet from which there is no visible sign of human beings.

If I sit for a while, then my impatience, crossness, frustration, are indeed annihilated, and my sense of humor returns.

Being a homemaker does not mean that you can't take time for yourself. In fact, women who have beaten housewife syndrome say that when they allow themselves, time to pursue personal goals or have some time to themselves, they have more energy for routine tasks and fewer physical and mental complaints. Housewife syndrome seems to disappear.

Along with developing interests outside of the home, take a few minutes to see how you can improve your job as a homemaker by creating a "Self Evaluation Chart."

1. List each of the activities you perform throughout the day. Incorporate tasks you do on a weekly or monthly basis at the end of the chart.

2. Next to each task, write down the amount of time it takes to complete it.

3. Fill in the name of the person who is benefiting from the activity. For example, next to cooking breakfast, you'd write "family" and next to mending a Little League uniform, you'd write your son's name, "Mark."

4. In the fourth column, rate the task from one to five using a "Value Scale." One is for those things you like to do—maybe cooking or going to the library. Five is for the things that are unpleasant for you—maybe driving carpools or holding Cub Scout meetings at your house.

5. In the final column, note which tasks could be shared with family members, swapped with friends, assigned to hired help, or performed less often. This step takes creativity. Don't just assume that you must continue to do everything the same way you've been doing it. And there may be a few things that you wouldn't mind doing more of if other tasks could be eliminated.

Just a few changes could make a difference in your disposition and the amount of free time you have during the week. For instance, if you don't mind cooking for parties but hate to hang wallpaper, why not swap chores with a friend who feels the opposite way. Offer to prepare the hors d'oeuvres for her next cocktail party if she'll re-paper your guest bathroom. Or if you detest ironing but love to sew, hire someone to do your ironing with the money you will save by making your own clothes.

Maybe you're driving carpools to school twice a week but realize that if your husband left ten minutes earlier, he could drive the kids to school on his way to work. And is there something you're trying to do when the kids are underfoot that could be done in less time after your husband gets home and can watch them?

If you hate the everyday drudgery of making dinner, consider making several days worth of food at once so that some can be frozen for those days when a quick meal is needed. And why not let those who are old enough attempt to cook or take their turn doing the grocery shopping? One woman with two teenage boys assigned each member of the family one week a month when he was responsible for grocery shopping. For the first few weeks they had to make early morning trips to the convenience store for oatmeal and bathroom tissue, but as soon as they realized their mother was serious, they began keeping a list of items as they ran low. Then on Thursday evenings, the person assigned to grocery shopping knew exactly what was needed.

OTHER OUTLETS

There's a lot to be said for women who used to take half an hour out of their mornings for a cup of coffee with a neighbor. Today's busier, mobile lifestyles and impersonal neighborhoods make that more difficult, yet housewives who take time to talk to one another—whether it's through an organized support group or regular chats on the phone—help each other find creative solutions to problems.

One group of women I know take their toddlers to the park every Friday morning from 9 to 11 a.m. While the kids play in the sandbox, the mothers share their feelings. "Career women aren't the only women who network," one of them told me.

Another group of five women have arranged their schedules so that twice a week four of the women go out to lunch while the fifth watches the children. "It's something to look forward to—a time to get dressed up and get out in the adult world," explained one mother.

And I have clients who have found other creative ways to overcome the housewife blues. Wanda, who loves gourmet cooking, began offering cooking classes to friends in her neighborhood. That not only gave her a creative outlet but provided money to save for family vacations and new clothes. And Charlotte enjoyed planning her daughter's wedding so much that she now offers her talents to other brides-to-be.

Another woman, Tricia, who was obsessed with buying clothes, realized that she was trying to fill a void in her life by shopping. Once she confronted her self-doubt, she realized that she really wanted to return to school. She talked it over with her husband and started attending law school two nights a week while he took care of their three-year-old. The couple also hired several high school girls to take turns babysitting for two hours each afternoon so Tricia could study.

MOTHERLY LOVE

Motherhood can be one of the most important roles a woman will ever play, but it doesn't have to be the only role. In fact, there are times when it's best if Mom finds her own interests apart from those of her husband and children.

Thirty-nine-year-old Kris had two daughters in junior high school when her son was ready to begin preschool. For three years, Kris had focused her attention on Daniel while her daughters were busy with school, Girl Scouts, and band practice. When the day came to enroll him, Kris considered keeping her son at home for another year.

"Then I remembered a sermon I heard twenty-two years ago," Kris recalls. "The minister said that parents often use their children to meet their own needs. He called it 'smotherly love.'"

"I didn't want to be the kind of mother who lived through her children or who wouldn't give them the independence they needed."

Kris enrolled Daniel in preschool and the same day walked into the Democratic campaign headquarters in her community to volunteer her time. "Housewives are good managers," says Kris. "My organizational abilities were immediately apparent, and I was able to apply to the campaign much of what I had learned from my husband's career in marketing."

After two years, Kris was asked to accept a paying job to organize a primary campaign for a school board official. Four years later, she was appointed director of public relations for a local hospital.

"When I went to my first meeting, I introduced myself by saying, 'Hi, I'm Kris Belmont, Director of Public Relations, but I used to be Donna Reed.' Other former full-time mothers knew what I meant. We all used to think that being a good wife, mother, lover, and Girl Scout leader was enough to make us feel worthwhile. While those roles are wonderful, homemakers also need to do things that make them feel needed for other non-domestic abilities and talents. I no longer saw myself as a chauffeur, baby sitter, or ornament on my husband's arm. I was Kris Belmont who, in addition to being a damn good mother and wife, had other skills and talents to offer the world."

THE EMPTY NEST

It is women who focus exclusively on their families for years who later suffer the most from the empty nest syndrome when their children leave home. When fifty-two-year-old Joan's youngest son left for college and to live on his own, she was overcome by a sense of isolation. Even though she had looked forward to this time when she and her husband would be free to do as they pleased, she found that she had many more empty hours a day to fill than she had expected.

While her husband Tom continued to work, Joan had no interests. There were no more high school PTA meetings to attend and no more proms to help plan. She considered getting a job, but she had no vocational skills. Even when her son and daughter came home from college for Christmas vacation, it was evident that they didn't need her as much as they had before. They had learned to do their own laundry and fix their own meals. Their lives were hectic and busy while hers was empty.

Joan needed to become involved in some type of activity to help fill the days. She joined a women's club and started playing golf with friends, but something was still missing from her life. Finally, she discussed her feelings with Tom.

"I need to feel useful again," Joan explained. "When the kids were home, I was always busy with one activity or the other. I never felt better than when I was planning the kids' proms."

"There's got to be something you can do that will enable you to use your talent to plan extravaganzas," said Tom. "Maybe we could open a small catering business."

Joan began investigating the catering businesses, but when she told the rabbi at her synagogue what she was doing her research ended.

"You can't open you're own business," the rabbi said. "We need you right here. We've just approved a position for a staff party planner to handle the bar mitzvahs and weddings we hold here, and I thought of you right away."

Two months later, Joan was working twenty hours a week at the temple. Her days were just the way she liked them—filled with things waiting to be done and with people who needed her and appreciated her talents.

When life seems to have no purpose, it's easy for doubt to take over and for housewife syndrome to flourish. Even women like Joan, who loved staying home to raise their children, must remember that they cannot give away their identity by living entirely through their families. It's important to find an activity that separates you from your family and reinforces your worth as an individual, whether it's an exercise or craft class, hospital volunteer work, or piano lessons. Being responsible for a family does not mean that you have to relinquish your personal goals and dreams.

BREAKING AWAY

Breaking out of the self-defeating housewife syndrome requires that you look at who you are and what you want to do with your life. When you decide to overcome your feelings of discouragement and hopelessness and renew your motivation, don't feel like you have to change all at once.

Use the "swiss cheese theory"—make small holes. You don't have to enroll immediately in a class or find a job. First, identify your needs and discover available alternatives. You need to take that first step to give you the momentum to lift you out of the doldrums. Then once you've decided what is right for you, you can begin to make positive changes.

Perhaps, after you evaluate the options, you'll realize that being a homemaker is what you like doing. There may be many enjoyable things that you would miss if you worked outside the home—like taking the kids to the park at midday, visiting friends, and pursuing hobbies.

These types of experiences can be fulfilling. But life as a housewife often looks unbearable to women who come to it with better educations and more developed social consciences than their grandmothers. Today's women live in a society that defines people by the prestige of what they do and how much money they earn, rather than by how much they enjoy what they're doing. It's important that we recognize what we like to do and the kind of person we want to be, rather than try to be what we think others expect us to be.

Some women who stay home full time and enjoy it pretend that it's not enough just so others will recognize that they have ambitions outside the home and take them more seriously. Many housewives feel embarrassed when businesswomen at their husband's office party ask them what they do for a living. I'd like to see a woman who is so free of self-doubt about her role as a homemaker that, when asked what she does, can say, "I cook, drive carpools, and am a terrific aerobic dancer. And it's a great way to spend my time!"

5

Self-Doubt on the Job

NEURASTHENIA does not only attack housewives. Career women and men are also victims. Instead of feeling trapped by their homes and families, working people feel stifled by boring jobs, dead-end positions, underemployment, and unappreciative bosses.

A twenty-five-year-old woman who lacks the education to get the job she really wants or a forty five-year-old man who is tired of the same workday routine are both victims of neurasthenia. But what ever the age, sex, or reason for feeling dissatisfied, working people often use the same excuses as housewives in order not to make desired changes. They tell themselves that they don't have the time, money, or ability to do anything different and convince themselves that they'll be stuck in the same rut forever.

The neurasthenic male feels dissatisfied with his life, unfulfilled by his work, and anxious about his future. He may have worked in the same field for years and now wants to find a new, more challenging career. He may have spent years trying, without success, to advance in a career and is now tired of striving without success. He may see more opportunity for making money in another line of work but thinks that it is too late in life to make a change. Or he may be tired of devoting so much time to work and want more time to play.

It is easy for a person contemplating a career change to be filled with doubt and question himself. "What if I fail? What if others don't approve of the change? What if my family isn't willing to sacrifice when I switch careers? What if I make a change and still am not satisfied?"

It sometimes seems easier to stay in an unfulfilling job or a boring career than to step into the unknown. But when we ignore our need to change, we eventually suffer.

KEVIN: A MAN IN CRISIS

After working seventeen years as an engineer for an aircraft manufacturer, Kevin, forty-four, was bored with his career. It became harder and harder to get up, go to work, and keep his mind on his job.

One day over lunch his friend, Jack, asked Kevin if he'd be interested in going into a partnership to buy a small seaside resort one hundred miles out of town. He convinced Kevin to drive up the coast that weekend to see the property.

The resort needed fresh paint and new landscaping, but Kevin hadn't felt so excited in months. During the drive home, he and Jack discussed how they would share the ownership responsibilities. Since Jack had a lucrative real estate business he didn't want to give up, Kevin would be responsible for the day-to-day management of the resort and receive a larger share of the profits.

Kevin sensed opportunity and a new freedom; it sounded like a dream come true. "And that's exactly what it will remain—a dream," Kevin's doubter interrupted his positive thoughts. "You have two kids and a wife to support. You can't change careers at this stage of your life."

Kevin's doubter immediately questioned Kevin's priorities. "How could you leave the security of your job for the unpredictability of a resort? Your wife and daughters don't want to move—they're comfortable where they are. They have friends and family closeby, not to mention their schools and the swim club. They'd never follow your pipe dream."

The more Kevin listened to his doubter, the more depressed he became. It was more difficult than ever to concentrate on his work. Finally, when his boss questioned his lack of motivation, Kevin knew he needed help to plan his future.

"I don't want to continue in my present job, but I'm afraid of making a mistake and jeopardizing my family's security," Kevin explained during a counseling session. "It feels like I'd be stepping out of a safe environment into a big, dark hole. There's no way of knowing what lies ahead. That frightens me."

Using the 10-step plan, Kevin thought about a time in the past when he felt similarly confused, at age sixteen when his parents divorced. "I've always viewed decisions in terms of right and wrong," he remembered, "so when my parents asked me to choose whom I wanted to live with, I was certain that only one choice could be the right one. I didn't want to let either parent down, so I avoided the decision and didn't say anything. When my father moved out and I stayed behind, the decision was made for me."

As Kevin continued with the ten steps, he described his doubter as a warrior dressed in heavy armor, complete with sword and shield. He named his doubter "Grendel."

"My doubter has been my protector and aggressor," said Kevin. "He's helped me to persevere—to get a good job, work hard, and earn promotions. But Grendel sees things only in terms of winning and losing. There's no room to make mistakes or accept new challenges. I'm tired of feeling like I'm fighting a battle between good and evil."

The reinforcer Kevin imagined was a powerful eagle, whom he called "Zoom." "Zoom has the strength to fly over mountains, the vision to see far and wide, the intelligence to anticipate the future appropriately, and the willingness to accept change," Kevin said.

Kevin knew that if he had had the reinforcer within him at age sixteen, he would have understood that every decision does not have to be final. If living with his mother didn't work out, he could have changed his mind and lived with his father. "Since my doubter tries to keep me in a two-dimensional world where there's only right and wrong, I believed that every decision I made was monumental. In addition, I only developed one side to my personality—that of the male provider who held a very traditional job. I kept any desires to try something different locked inside."

Weeks later, Kevin was able to realize how the reinforcer could work in his life. "I'm beginning to see that I have a more creative side that will allow me to explore new territory, take chances, and be more open to change," he said. "I want to shed my old notions about what men are supposed to do and give myself room to explore less traditional career options."

Several months later Kevin announced he was going to become a partner in the resort. "My family doesn't want to move, but that doesn't mean I have to give up my dream. I'm going to commute back and forth a few times a week, and they're going to spend several weekends a month at the resort with me," he explained. "And if the situation doesn't work out, that doesn't mean I failed. I reevaluate and try again."

Many men today are evaluating old standards in their careers, lifestyles, and relationships. Kevin had to realize that being a man didn't mean that he had to work in the same job until he retired. He needed to see that once he achieved one goal, he could move on to others.

If you spend your life trying to please other people, you never get a chance to explore your own interests and fulfill your goals. Don't ignore needs because your doubter tells you that they're unimportant. And don't abandon dreams because your doubter says they're unattainable. Use the 10-step plan to evaluate your feelings and their origins, and then determine the adjustments you can make so that the reinforcer within you can help you discover new feelings of satisfaction, reward, and success.

LISA: HELD BACK BY HER BOSS

Lisa, thirty-five, is an account executive for a small marketing firm. She is married and has a ten-year-old daughter. Her family depends on her salary as much as on that of her husband.

"My problem is that I love the field I'm in and earn a good salary, but I can't stand my boss," Lisa explained. "I want to perform to my fullest, but my boss holds me back. She's very busy and disorganized, but won't give me any responsibility or let me do what I do best—plan and organize.

"I feel trapped and anxious, so to cope I smoke and eat twice as much as I should," Lisa continued. "I can't get to sleep at night because I know that I'll have to go right back to that craziness in the morning."

Lisa remembered times when she was young and she felt the same way. "My mother's favorite words for me were 'imbecile' and 'stupid.' Her opinion of me made me doubt my abilities. Every time I had to take a test in junior high and high school, I became so nervous that I felt like I couldn't breathe. Later in life, I'd get the same feeling on job interviews, first dates, or in any unfamiliar situation. The only person I remember who encouraged me was my home economics teacher. She said I was an excellent student and recommended me for several awards."

Lisa described the doubting side of her as a woman who looks just like she does, but who is encased in a block of ice. "My doubter is gasping for air, as if she's just about to suffocate."

Lisa named her doubter "Ice." When asked how her doubter had worked for her in the past, she explained, "By being icy and cold, my doubter has helped me to size up situations without getting emotionally involved. So it's helped me to make level headed decisions. But I'm tired of being a victim of my doubter's icy ways. She freezes me from taking action."

Lisa's reinforcer looks identical to her doubter, but it's surrounded with warmth and sunshine. "My reinforcer, whom I'll call 'Sunshine,' acts more self-assured than my doubter," says Lisa. "She's peaceful and confident—the way I felt when my home economics teacher praised me."

When asked how her creative side could help her to confront her doubts, Lisa explained, "The stress of working in a confining job for an unappreciative boss caused me to suffer physically as well as mentally. I developed severe migraine headaches and stomach problems. Subconsciously I must want to be sick because then I won't have to work for a boss I don't like and can't respect.

"I want Sunshine to teach me how to relax, how to remain calm, and to stand up for what I feel is right. She will help me come up with well-thought out-decisions and behave rationally. She will remind me that I'm not alone and cold—that there is sunshine all around me."

Lisa used her creative side to develop a few solutions to her problems at work. She decided to try, for six months, to make changes at work. She would begin to tell her boss about the kind of support and responsibility she, Lisa, needed to do a better job. By the end of that time, if her relationship with her boss had not improved, she would begin looking for a new job.

"I can't be a victim any longer," she said. "If I had known

about my reinforcer when I was younger, I would have asked my mother not to call me names. Tests, interviews, and dates would have been a challenge, not a burden. I would have known that I was intelligent and bright and that it was me—not a test score, not a job, not a boy—that had the power to make me feel good about myself."

EVALUATING CHANGE

Before you let dreams slip away, stay in unhealthy situations, or jump too quickly at new challenges, take time to assess your needs and desires. Before you make a decision, ask yourself the following questions to help you understand the source of your doubt and to evaluate your options:

Why am I considering making the change?

For whom am I making the change? (Myself, my parents, my spouse, my children?)

If I'm changing for someone else, is it for a good reason or because I'm trying to prove something or live up to his expectations? (Moving to a new city because your spouse will have an opportunity to advance in his/her career may be a good reason to make a change, but accepting a new job just because it will look good to the neighbors is not a good reason.)

How important is the change to me? Is there something else that might make me feel just as good?

If I make this change, what will I give up? What will I gain?

It's not easy to learn to trust your decision-making ability. You have to pay close attention to what your body and mind are telling you. Kevin's first clue that he needed a new career challenge was his feeling of depression. Later, after he had a taste of a new opportunity, his doubter tried to discourage him from buying the resort. But when his disinterest in work persisted to the point that it affected his performance, he knew that it was time to face his feelings.

Your instincts are often a good barometer of how you really feel about a certain situation. Decisions become more difficult to make when you let other people's opinions or social norms weigh more heavily in your life than how you feel.

Lisa's doubter prevented her from dealing effectively with problems at work. Instead of telling her boss about how she felt or suggesting ways the office could be run more efficiently, Lisa kept her frustration inside and became physically ill. She had felt the same way when her mother had called her an "imbecile" or "stupid" and she had not stood up for herself. But when she realized that she no longer had to accept that negative picture of herself, she began to take action, confront her boss and avoid further illness.

The mind and the body are not separate. Ulcers, colitis, migraine headaches, hypertension, heart problems, colds, and flus are often caused or intensified by psychological fears and inward-directed anger. Like Lisa, we have to learn how to express our feelings in a constructive way and know when it's time to get out of a potentially harmful work situation.

When dealing with a difficult person, try not to blame him for how you're feeling, but let him know what's bothering you. Instead of using statements like, "You make me feel awful," try "I feel bad when this happens," or "In the future, I'd prefer if it happened this way..."

Change seldom comes easily or without mistakes. We learn from mistakes. Don't dwell on them. Determine where you went wrong and then attempt to keep moving forward and try to avoid the same mistakes in the future.

6

"Marriage Will Make Me Happy" and Other Myths

BEING married today is probably more difficult than at any previous time. The steps we've taken toward equality in marriage have caused husbands and wives to expect more from each other than ever before.

Women want men to share in the housework, spend more time with the family, show more emotion and be more sensitive. At the same time, they want men to be agressive and successful in their careers. And although most women say they want their husbands to put their families first, few would want their spouses to take a year off work to be househusbands. Husbands are expected to have the wonderful traits of the sensitive, caring men of the eighties and all of the good—and none of the bad—characteristics of their less liberated fathers.

It's not just women who have demands. Today's men expect more, too. Those who have working wives often depend on their spouses' incomes. Yet despite full-time jobs, wives are still expected to be responsible for the housework and organizing the family's social life.

I know few men who are married to full-time homemakers who offer to help with the housework. And many feel put out when, after a tiring day at work, they are expected to watch the kids while their wives go to dance classes and computer courses.

The role of husbands and wives may be less defined than they were twenty years ago, but they are more demanding. While we say we have new attitudes, we have not let old expectations die.

The following myths about marriage have lingered, despite enlightened views, high divorce rates, and second marriages, in which couples often have more realistic expectations. After each myth, I've listed common, potentially dangerous, doubts that develop when the marriage doesn't live up to the expectation created by the myth. You may be experiencing some of these doubts today. Others may not affect you now but may be of concern to you at a future time. Finally, I've described a more realistic picture of marriage and offered suggestions on how to work out doubts that can threaten a relationship.

I have created a mythical couple, John and Mary (based on couples I've treated), to use as an example of how believing the myths can affect a marriage. Examples of how John and Mary worked through trouble spots in their relationship and additional suggestions for overcoming marital problems that stem from buying the myths are offered.

MYTH 1: MARRIAGE WILL MAKE ME HAPPY

DOUBTS: I'm not happy; I shouldn't stay married.

I must be a bad spouse.

I should be happier.

REALITY: Most people marry to fill needs for love, companionship, and emotional support. While marriage may fill many needs, it cannot fill all of them. In fact, marriage often complicates life by adding new issues to be resolved and compromises to be made.

Many people expect their husbands or wives to help them recover from failures and disappointments they've experienced in the past. But one person cannot make up for a lack of love and support we suffered in our childhood or for the frustrations we've experienced with family, friends, and employers.

Contrarily, those who were raised by loving, caring parents, expect their spouses to give them that type of encouragement once they're married. But if those partners didn't have a supportive family, it may take years before they learn how to be the supportive spouses their partners need and expect—or they may never be able to change.

WORKING OUT THE DOUBT: Sharing your life with someone can be wonderful, but no one person can be responsible for your complete happiness, nor should he or she be expected to be.

If you're unhappy and think your marriage is to blame, ask

what constitutes a happy marriage. Then compare your expectation of marriage to your existing relationship and determine ways in which you can create the type of marriage you desire.

Before you develop a strategy for change, identify any biases that cause you to have unrealistic expectations. For example, Mary was unhappy because she thought that she and John argued too much. Her idea of an acceptable level of disagreement was directly related to her parent's behavior toward one another. Mary rarely saw her parents argue, so she viewed any amount of disagreement as a sign of an unhappy marriage. Yet, other people who had parents who argued a lot and eventually divorced may think that any amount of disagreement spells divorce.

An essential element to working out marital problems is to let your spouse know what you want. Too often, people complain to their partners about their behavior before taking the time to tell their mates how they would prefer that they behave.

Once Mary understood why she felt the way she did, she analyzed the source of her and John's arguments and realized that the majority of their fights were about the household chores. Before the next argument erupted, she asked John to work with her to negotiate an agreement to split the work.

During the conversation, Mary let John know how she felt about his lack of help around the house and how she wanted him to change. Instead of using "you" messages like, "You never clean the bathroom," Mary used "I" messages such as, "I think it would be fair if you and I took turns cleaning the bathroom every other week." The "I" messages clearly stated what Mary wanted without threatening or accusing John.

MYTH 2: MY SPOUSE WILL CHANGE AFTER WE'RE MARRIED

DOUBTS: He hasn't changed so he doesn't love me.

I can't change her;

I'm a failure.

REALITY: Behavior is fixed at a very early age. No amount of love on either side can make someone change if that person does not feel the need to. We may want our spouses to change, but they may be happy as they are. Sometimes a crisis, such as marital separation, a death in the family, or the threat of losing a job may cause a person to change, but even then the motivation must come from within.

WORKING OUT THE DOUBT: Analyze which of your spouse's behaviors are not acceptable to you. Then determine why your spouse acts that way. Try to understand how your partner's childhood caused certain characteristics to develop.

Arrange a time when you and your spouse can discuss the reasons that you feel change is necessary, and be sure to let him or her offer a point of view. Try to work out a compromise so that neither of you loses.

Mary felt that John should be more interested in her work. Typically she would talk nonstop about her work from the time she got home until they went to bed, hoping John would show interest and becoming frustrated because he didn't. When Mary stopped to analyze John's behavior, she realized that he was "tuning her out," the same way John's father responded to his mother's constant chatter.

With this insight, Mary asked John if he would take ten minutes each evening to talk about her day, if, in exchange, she did the same for him. During those ten minutes, Mary was assured of John's undivided attention.

With some work you may be able to change a person's behavior, but you will not change the person. You cannot make an introvert into an extrovert or turn a worrier into a carefree spirit, but you can help your partner take small, mutually agreed-upon steps that will enhance your relationship.

MYTH 3: THE MORE MY SPOUSE IS WITH ME, THE MORE HE LOVES ME

DOUBTS: He spends so much time at work;
he must not love me.

She spends so much time with friends;
our marriage must be failing.

REALITY: The amount of time a couple spends together is not proportionate to the amount of love that couple shares. A balance of togetherness and time apart often results in a more satisfying relationship. When spouses have time to explore separate interests, they often put more value on the time they spend together and are able to enliven that time with fresh conversation and new points of view.

There may be times in a relationship when a partner must spend time away from home, such as when a spouse starts a new business or returns to school. But if the partner continues to spend an excessive amount of time away from home once the business is underway or the school semester is over, it may be time to discuss alternatives or seek professional help.

WORKING OUT THE DOUBT: The first thing to do if you feel slighted by your mate is to ask yourself why you're unhappy. Do you really feel that you and your partner need more time together, or are you dissatisfied with your own lifestyle and jealous of the fulfillment your partner finds in his?

If you seem to be more disturbed by your own lack of interests than by your spouse's lack of attention, take time to find more satisfying ways to fill your time. Are there hobbies you could pursue? Classes you could take? Friends you could see more often? If you're satisfied with your life, but still feel that you and your spouse need more time together, tell your partner how you feel. But don't air your frustrations and then wait for a miracle. If you want things to change, take the initiative and make the change happen.

As a two-career couple, Mary and John spend many evenings and weekends involved in work-related projects. After complaining for months that they needed to spend more time together, Mary told John how unhappy she was. She asked if they could arrange their schedules to spend at least one night a week and half a day on the weekends together doing something fun or relaxing. She also suggested that they go to bed together half an hour earlier so that they could have some private time on a daily basis.

Sometimes, a spouse may spend an inordinate amount of

time at work or with friends to avoid confronting problems at home. Each person in a relationship has limits for the type of behavior he is willing to accept from his partner. If Mary objects to John spending three nights a week playing racquetball, she needs to tell him that she can no longer continue in the relationship as it is and then ask him to change his behavior. Mary may suggest that they make an agreement to try to work out their problems by themselves for a month or two. If in that time they can't, they should agree to receive professional help. If John is unwilling to change or to seek help, Mary may need to end the relationship. To thrive, a marriage needs goodwill—the willingness to do things for one another.

MYTH 4: YOUR SUCCESS IS ALL I NEED

DOUBTS: I'm worth nothing without her.
If he doesn't succeed, we both fail.
I don't have any interest of my own.

REALITY: If you place more importance on your partner's worth than on your own, your self-esteem may be in jeopardy. There are very few people who can continue to feel good about themselves if their partners constantly receive positive recognition and they receive little, if any.

WORKING OUT THE DOUBT: Spouses must develop their own feelings of self-worth. Traditionally, women more often than men have based their sense of self-worth on their husbands' accomplishments. And it was those women who often had the most difficult time coping with their new lives when they separated or divorced, when their husbands died, or when their spouses quit prestigious jobs. Women often stayed in unhappy marriages for years rather than lose status by leaving their husbands.

A study conducted by Donald Lammers, Ph.D., of Dallas, Texas, showed that husbands and wives differed considerably in how they responded to each other's self-doubt.[4] "If a husband says, 'Gee, I don't know what to do,' the wife often becomes anxious," says Dr. Lammers. "Women want to perceive their husbands as competent, successful, in control, and able to take care of them. But if the wife expressed self-doubt, the husband typically did not become anxious. In fact, he often felt more in control."

While it's important for spouses to support each other, it is equally important for them to create their own plans and goals. Mary's moods fluctuate with John's. If he's happy in his job, she's happy. If he has a good game of racquetball, she feels good. But when John is discouraged at work or loses a game, Mary feels like a loser, too.

Mary's feelings of self-worth should come from her own achievements. She should not use other people's yardsticks, not even John's, to measure her success. While John may receive his feelings of self-worth from the recognition he gets at work or from winning a racquetball game, hers may come from volunteering time to a child-abuse prevention program or selling an oil painting to a gallery.

Mary cannot ignore her own needs and desires. She must recognize and accept her own authority, set goals, and work toward them. And while she will probably discuss her personal goals with John, she should not wait for his permission before she pursues them. Mary needs to learn to trust her feelings. By doing that she will reinforce her feelings of self-worth.

MYTH 5: HAVING CHILDREN WILL SOLVE OUR PROBLEMS

DOUBTS: What if we have children but still have problems?

Our marriage has problems;
children must not be filling our needs.

REALITY: Having a child can enrich a solid relationship, but the new demands a child makes on parents' time and energy can create extra problems and can damage a faltering marriage. People who want a child to solve their marital problems often expect the child to provide the love and affection that they don't get from one another. But having a child for that reason is unfair; it places too many expectations on the child, who can't possibly make up for an unfulfilling marriage.

WORKING OUT THE DOUBT: John and Mary want a child to draw them closer together, but instead of looking to children to make their relationship better, they need to tackle their problems head on. Their need for better communication, a more satisfying sex life, companionship, or any of a number of other things may be disguised as a need for a child. Since a child will add a new level of responsibility, they should work to make their relationship as strong as possible before having a child.

If once they have a child, their marital problems continue, John and Mary should not use the child as a scapegoat. Parents need to identify the source of their frustrations and work together to solve it, not look for someone or something to blame.

MYTH 6: WE ONLY ARGUE ABOUT MONEY—THAT'S NOT REALLY IMPORTANT

DOUBTS: I have to ask before I buy anything;
I feel like a child.

I am not good enough to get what I want.

Money is more important to my partner than I am.

REALITY: When couples argue about money, the source of their disagreement usually runs deeper than a new pair of shoes or a new car. Conflicts over money often revolve around issues of control, power, and dominance in a relationship as well as a need for individuality and separateness.[5]

WORKING OUT THE DOUBT: Look at the hidden messages of hurt, anger, disappointment that may be causing arguments about money. Do you have to ask for permission to spend money? Does your partner expect you to spend less money than he does because you earn less? Is it the money or the feeling of powerlessness that bothers you?

Mary makes less money than John, so she feels guilty whenever she spends money on clothes for herself. She hates the thought of asking for permission to spend money, but John seems irritated when she buys a new dress. "I spend more than John on clothes, but he buys more expensive toys," says Mary. "Last year, he bought a three-wheel motorcycle to ride in the desert with friends. I could have bought fifty dresses for that amount of money!"

John and Mary may want to consider resolving their conflicts over how to spend "extra" money by paying household bills out of a joint account and putting spending money for clothes, recreation and entertainment into two separate accounts. Both John and Mary should be allotted the same amount of money each month and should have the freedom to spend it however they see fit. If Mary were a housewife and did not bring home a paycheck, she should still be given the same amount of spending money as John.

Some couples believe that the partner who earns more should have more spending money. But that kind of arrangement can lead to resentment, especially if the spouse who makes less money sacrificed his career to help the other advance professionally. A marriage works best when the emphasis is not on the amount of money each partner earns but on the effort each makes to enhance the relationship.

How a partner handles money in a relationship is often subconsciously equated with giving and with-holding love. Couples who find ways to solve money problems often are able to solve many other issues that involve the division of power.

MYTH 7: YOUR SEXUAL FRUSTRATION IS NOT MY FAULT

DOUBTS: I'm not sexually attractive enough.

We wouldn't have this problem if he loved me.

The rest of our relationship will suffer because of our problems in bed.

REALITY: Couples often believe that sexual problems are unrelated to other marital problems. But the general state of the marriage is more responsible than anything for the amount of satisfaction couples experience from intimacy and sex.

WORKING OUT THE DOUBT: Communication is the best way to resolve sexual problems. Although partners should let each other know their desires during lovemaking, discussing sexual problems at that time can be emotionally damaging and can take away the spontaneity. It's best to discuss sexual problems outside of the bedroom where both partners can approach the subject rationally and without feeling threatened.

John and Mary have problems telling each other what pleases them. They should discuss their needs and fantasies and tell each other what arouses them and what turns them off.

In long-term relationships, couples have to work to keep the romantic spark alive. They can consider setting aside time to be alone and creating a romantic atmosphere. A candlelit dinner, a bubble bath, or even a new perfume can create new interest.

For more serious problems, such as impotence, premature ejaculation, or a continual lack of affection, it's usually best to seek professional help, either individually or as a couple.

MYTH 8: IF WE LOVE EACH OTHER, THINGS WILL ALWAYS WORK OUT

DOUBT: We can't agree; we must not love each other.

I'm always giving in; I must be weak.

He won't give in; he must not love me.

REALITY: Divorce statistics prove that the "love conquers all" theory is an over-assessment of what love can do to hold a marriage together. Just because two people love each other does not mean that they will not disagree. Nor does it mean that they will be able to work out conflicts in a way that satisfies them both.

"People feel guilty when they fight because they think that

happily married couples shouldn't fight," says Dr. Lammers, whose study looks at how couples negotiate marital conflicts. "It seems to help a relationship when couples learn to openly disagree and air some of their hostility. My research shows that differences need not be resolved to have an affectionate relationship, only that the couple be comfortable enough to argue with each other. The denial or fear of anger and arguments seems to surpress affection.

"Couples need to realize that differences are not an indication that their marriage is a failure. In fact, it's almost impossible for people to live in total harmony, and there may be points on which spouses never agree," Dr. Lammers continues. "Spouses should be able to tolerate, even enjoy their differences and the occasional tension that results. That spark of tension can often keep a relationship more alive than scheduled dinners or 'talks.'"[6]

WORKING OUT THE DOUBT: When you and your partner can't agree, realize that just because two people live together and love each other does not mean that they should think and react alike. Sometimes you may have to make a decision without your partner's consent.

Mary needs to go on a business trip, but John doesn't want her to go. Mary should evaluate the circumstances, and if she feels that she must go on the trip, she should tell John why the trip is important to her. Mary should let John know that even though she is going against his wishes, she doesn't love him any less.

Because of the trip, John had to cancel a dinner engagement with friends. To make up for the spoiled plans, Mary can arrange another get-together. Sometimes, however, there is no way to make up for hurt feelings. One spouse may feel slighted and the other may feel guilty, but each has to make a decision that seems appropriate at the time. Unfortunately, life does not always work itself out in ways that make both partners happy. The important thing is to not dwell on disagreements. Move on and be as encouraging and loving as possible.

Myth 9: Divorce Will Solve My Problems

DOUBTS: If I divorce my spouse, I'm a failure.
No one will love me again.
I'll never be able to support myself if we divorce.
My children will suffer if we divorce,
so I'll stay in an unhappy relationship.

REALITY: There are many reasons why relationships end: couples grow in different directions; circumstances (money, health, careers) change radically; or one spouse meets a more compatible person. Often divorce occurs because of problems one or both partners have with self-esteem; when you can't see much good in yourself, you can't see much good in others either.

While divorce is sometimes the best alternative when two people cannot get along or no longer enjoy one another, it will not solve all of a person's problems. In fact, the divorce process and the feelings of guilt, resentment and fear that follow divorce often do as much to harm a person's self-esteem as the unhappy marriage.

And just because a relationship ends doesn't mean that it didn't suit a couple's needs at one time, nor does it mean that one or both partners failed. Yet people who divorce develop serious doubts about themselves, their abilities to be good spouses in the future, and their capacity to love.

When divorce or separation occurs, it's easy to transfer feelings of inadequacy from your marriage to other areas of your life. And when you've put all your trust and hope into a relationship that doesn't last, there's a tendency, at first, to want not to trust any one again.

WORKING OUT THE DOUBT: It's never easy to get over divorce, but to go on when it happens, you must learn from the experience. Identify the problems you had in your marriage and try to avoid repeating the same mistakes in the future. It's always easy to look back at a relationship and to identify what went wrong and what you could have done. If you had known then what you know now, you might have done things differently. Accept the mistakes you made and move on, remembering that you have a chance to act differently in the future.

DISPELLING THE MYTHS

For years people have believed these marriage myths and have used them to measure the success of their marriages. When their expectations were not met, they became disillusioned and their marriages suffered.

Marriage partners must respect each other as well as themselves. If you can begin to control your self-doubt and your partner can do the same, your chances for a healthy marriage will increase dramatically and you'll discover new capabilities and areas for growth, both individually and as a couple.

The best way to overcome doubt in a marriage is through communication, with each partner spending equal time listening and speaking. Even if you don't agree with your spouse, realize that his or her feelings are important. Be interested in what is said and ask questions to be sure that you understand him or her. Only through communication can you and your spouse create the kind of marriage that will work for both of you.

7

LITTLE ONES CAN HAVE BIG FEARS: HELP FOR CHILDREN AND TEENS

"I HAVE very few self-doubts because my parents gave me a great foundation of love and emotional support," says Los Angeles Raiders running back Marcus Allen. "They taught me it's important to dream and to work hard to make my dreams materialize.

"You have to believe in yourself," continues the twenty-six-year-old Heisman trophy winner. "The other day I looked in the mirror and said, 'Boy, you look good.' A friend teased me about being vain, but I smiled and said, 'If nobody else is going to tell me I look good, I'm gonna tell myself.' I don't consider myself vain, I just want to keep striving to be the best I can be."

If only all children could be raised to have that kind of self-esteem. We then wouldn't have to wonder whether our children will grow up to be content, productive, well-adjusted adults. A child's self-image begins forming immediately after birth from the signals he receives from his parents. While most of what parents bring to their children's lives is good, parents also unintentionally pass along the insecurities and doubts they inherited from their own mothers and fathers.

Unfortunately, parents receive little or no training on how to minimize a child's self-doubt. Parents must understand that a very young child does not know how to decipher and analyze the messages he receives. He does not know that he is separate and different from his parents. Parents are the most powerful force in a small child's life. If a parent tells a child he is stupid, ugly, or ungrateful, he grows up thinking that he is stupid, ugly, or ungrateful.

Judi's parents constantly told her that she was a spoiled brat. Today, at age thirty-seven, she still feels like a bad little girl. "I was an only child, and my parents gave me everything I wanted," she says. "They didn't know how to set limits for me. I would have been better off if they had told me 'No' once in a while, rather than giving me so much and then blaming me for being spoiled. I've spent much of my adult life telling myself that I don't deserve things that I often don't even try to succeed."

HOW PARENTS AND KIDS CAN OVERCOME OBSTACLES

This chapter is not meant to blame our parents for our shortcomings or to instill guilt and fear in today's parents. Instead, it is intended to be a tool to help build a child's self-worth from this moment on.

Marcus Allen developed self-repect because of the examples set at home. "When things didn't go right, my parents didn't put me down," he remembers. "They told me that there'd be good days and bad days. I learned that when things went wrong, I had to pick myself up, dust myself off, and tell myself that I'd do better tomorrow."

Allen's self-image is immediately apparent when he describes the reinforcer within him. "I'm a knight in shining armor," the football player says without hesitation. And what about when his doubter creeps in? "My armor get a little bit tarnished," he admits, "but there's polish and I shine myself up and go out again."

Just like many kids today, Allen has felt pressure to use alcohol and drugs, both in school and professional sports. But the messages his parents gave him helped him not to succumb to this peer pressure.

"I can honestly say that I never smoked a joint, used cocaine, or tried any other drug," Allen says. "I've been drunk twice, and it was the worst feeling I've ever had. My father used to tell my brothers and me that if we wanted alcohol, we were to tell him. We knew he didn't want us to drink, but if we were going to, he wanted it to be in our home."

Children today are growing up even faster than when Allen

was young. Many elementary school students are dealing with pressures that their parents didn't have to confront until high school or college, including drugs, sex, violence, their parents' divorce, and keeping in step with fashion trends.

Kids need parents to spend time with them to give them direction and reinforcement. But to provide their children with positive experiences, parents must remove obstacles that prevent them from giving this support. The obstacles are different for each parent. For many mothers and fathers, the primary roadblock is their attitude toward life. It's hard to be good role models if we're always speaking negatively around our children. How can children develop self-esteem if parents are constantly complaining or denigrating themselves?

To feel good about yourself and the time you spend with your child, you must first confront your own doubts and fears. Only then will you become more aware of how what you say and do affects your child's self-image.

You'll have a more positive attitude toward your child if you take care of yourself as well as your family. Make arrangements to take brief personal retreats—time to read the newspaper, to have a glass of wine and talk to your spouse, or to soak in the bathtub.

Another major obstacle for parents is finding creative and effective ways to use time. We often create lists of "shoulds" that are really less important than having time to ourselves or with our families. What does your list look like? Are there any items you can eliminate?

Do you have to do all the housework yourself? Don't be afraid to ask for help either from your family, a neighborhood teenager who wants to earn extra money, or a professional housekeeper.

Do you have an offer to serve on both the school board and the church board? Determine how much time each takes and whether you can really afford, emotionally, to do both.

Do you have to polish the silver, fill the cookie jar with homemade cookies, and maintain a flower garden? Are you doing such things because you like to do them or because you feel you should?

It doesn't hurt a child to be given responsibilities, even at a young age. In fact, it instills values such as independence and family cooperation. Children who grow up in families that share housework develop a better understanding of the kind of support a family needs to thrive. If Mom wouldn't dare pay a bill and Dad wouldn't think of touching a vacuum, kids grow up believing that business is men's work and housework is women's work, and they have a hard time accepting anything different.

Consider making a list of the work each family member needs to complete during the week. It's often best to rotate chores so that one person does not have to do something he hates for weeks at a time. A simple written contract that states the task and the reward will help children understand the importance of their work. The contract might say, "If John takes the trash out every night, he will earn a two-dollar allowance." Then, if John does not live up to his side of the agreement, he will understand why he doesn't earn all of his allowance.

Holding weekly family meetings to update one another on accomplishments and plans also helps to build goodwill and interest among family members. The more we know, the less fear and anxiety we have. Parents should discuss with children only those plans that they are mature enough to understand. Discussing details about finances or work problems can put too much pressure and a false sense of responsibility on a child.

Another major problem parents face is knowing how to react to problems that arise during a child's life—such as toilet training, sharing toys and other possessions, bedwetting, misbehaving at school, and competition in sports. How a parent approaches a child's problems has a direct effect on how well the child overcomes the problem.

Children usually weather problems better and keep their self-esteem intact when parents help them create solutions rather than forcing solutions upon them. Parents should encourage and reinforce but not push. Kids who are pushed too hard often grow up feeling that they cannot control their own lives and, in turn, are often not able to make decisions or support other people in their lives.

Talking with your child is the best way to find out why a

problem is occurring. If a child wets the bed at night, the parents first need to understand that the bedwetting may be an expression of anger or fear. Rather than chastising or embarrassing the child, the parents should ask the child about the problem and try to discover what is happening in their child's life that might be triggering the problem. If the problem persists, however, professional help may be necessary.

A child's behavior is usually a clue to what is happening in his world. The behavior is a symptom, not the cause, of the problem. Try to spend some time alone with the child. Ask him how he is feeling about himself, school, friends, and home life.

Here are a few questions that might help you determine the problem:

Are you mad about anything?

How are things going at school?

What is your teacher(s) like?

What do you think about the other kids in the class?

Do you think Mom and Dad are nice to each other? To you?

How do you feel about your brothers and sisters?

What do you wish could happen?

HELPING YOUR CHILD USE THE 10-STEP PLAN

Children over the age of eight usually can benefit by taking part in the 10-step plan. Parents may want to explain each step to their child and then help him review and interpret his answers. The plan can help the child and parents understand how the circumstances in the child's life are affecting how he feels about himself. It can also identify areas in which a child needs special attention.

Children will respond to the formula differently from adults. Their answers will not be as detailed, and they cannot remember as much of the past as adults can. Some children may feel intimidated if asked to complete the ten steps with their parents. Often a friend, relative, or counselor—someone less involved in the child's life—can be a good, objective listener.

Adam is a fourteen-year-old who completed the 10-step plan with his parents. When asked to describe an area in his life that was causing him to experience self-doubt, Adam answered, "So much emphasis at school is placed on being popular. Sometimes, I don't do what I want to do if I think I won't look 'in,' and that makes me mad."

Thinking back to an earlier time when he felt the same way, Adam remembered how he felt when he and two close friends were struggling to see who was most popular. "Alan, Pete, and I were always trying to see who was on top." Adam recalls. "Now that I look back, I see how stupid that was. But at that time I had doubts about my popularity, so I went along with it. We'd see who could do the best in sports, who could be the funniest, and who could win the girls' attention."

Adam described the doubter within him as a dark shape. "It's dark like fear," he said. "It's how I feel when I do something that other kids don't think is 'in.'"

Asked how his doubter has helped him in the past, Adam thought for a minute and said, "It has helped me to become aware of how I respond to situations—like how I avoid doing things because of what I think other kids will think of me. My doubter holds me back, but later I can sit back and see what I could have done if I hadn't been so afraid."

Adam wanted to make some changes in his life. "I wish I would have run for an office in the student government last year," he said. "I didn't because none of my friends were running, and I was afraid they'd make fun of me."

Adam was willing to discover the reinforcer within himself to help him make those changes. "My reinforcer is a light color—it's kind of free-flowing and loose," Adam explained. "I think my reinforcer can help me realize that if I really want to do something I shouldn't be held back just because of what other people might think. I guess I can take more chances."

And how could Adam have used his reinforcer in the past when he and his friends were trying to prove their popularity? "I could have accepted that some things I wanted to do wouldn't be considered 'in.' And I would have spoken up and told my friends how stupid I thought it all was."

Adam's parents helped him to summarize his feelings. "What you're saying is that you have to trust yourself more, is that right?" his mother asked.

"Yeah," Adam answered. "I think that I had such a poor baseball season last year because I was playing with a new team, and I thought I was the underdog. I doubted myself from the first day of the season. This year I'm not going to let mistakes get me down. I'm going to believe in myself."

"Good," his dad encouraged. "Remember that the doubter and reinforcer are always with you. When the darker side of you doubts your ability or tries to win other people's approval, the lighter side of you is there, too. Tell yourself that you have ability and that you don't have to do just what appears in.

Do what seems right for you."

A year after Adam created his doubter and reinforcer, I asked him how they had impacted his life.

"I'm not sure. I haven't really thought about my doubter and reinforcer for a long time," Adam said. He paused briefly, then added, "Well, wait a minute. Maybe I have been using them without even thinking about it. I have had a totally different attitude than I had before I discovered my doubter and reinforcer. I feel more confident and don't worry as much about what people think about me."

Like most people who have completed the 10-step plan, Adam doesn't always consciously think about using his doubter and reinforcer, but that doesn't mean they don't help him keep his doubts in perspective. Through the use of the visualization technique presented in the 10 steps, the doubter and reinforcer have become synthesized into Adam's subconscious and are now a natural part of his modus operandi.

BALANCING DISCIPLINE AND ENCOURAGEMENT

It's not easy for a parent to know how to balance discipline, encouragement, and affection. One way to gauge yourself is to answer the following questions and then evaluate how you interact with your child:

Have you set realistic expectations and boundaries and discussed them with your child?

Are you treating your child with love and respect?

Do you expect your child to follow in your footsteps or to be what you never had a chance to be?

Do you praise your child when he deserves it?

When a child's behavior is unacceptable, do you remember to reject the behavior, not the child?

It's sometimes hard for parents to understand how something that seems insignificant to them can be so important to their child or teenager. Before you react to what your child does and says, remember that growing up is filled with periods of change, confusion, and, by adult standards, irrational thinking. Try to remember what was important to you when you were your child's age, so you can respond to your child's emotions and needs with compassion and understanding.

Above all, children need love and respect. They are individuals who have rights to their opinions, ideals, and privacy. Children do not need parents to police them and force them to be what their parents want them to be. They need parents to love, guide and discipline them so that they can learn how to effectively cope with problems, interact with others, enjoy life, and develop their own potential.

8

How Jealousy and Envy Affect Self-Esteem

LAST year Todd, a Chicago attorney, met two former college classmates in Mazatlan, Mexico, the scene of a gloriously carefree spring vacation some years earlier. Todd came home from the reunion with a golden tan, but green with envy. The trip had been more of a source of irritation than a time to relax and rekindle old friendships. For days after he returned, Todd belittled his friend, Ron pointing out his shortcomings and saying that Ron's success had been "just luck." Yet Todd said hardly a word about Bruce, the other member of the trio.

"Why are you always putting down Ron?" Todd's wife asked. "I'd think you'd be closer to him than you are to Bruce. You two have so much in common."

"He's doing everything I want to do," Todd confessed. "He's already a partner in his firm; I'm not. His cases are much more interesting than mine. And to top it all off, he just bought a new sports car. I'm still driving the car I drove in law school. I guess I'm just envious."

"But Bruce has done extremely well as a film director," his wife pointed out. "Why do you compare yourself to him?" "I don't know. He just received a first place award at a film festival, and he's buying a thirty-two-foot sailboat. I'm happy for him, but I guess those aren't things I want."

Like Todd, most of us envy people who have what we want or are doing something we'd like to do. When someone's success reminds us of what we thought we could do, but haven't tried, or makes our attempts to achieve the same goal seem inferior, envy often creeps in. The minute we compare ourselves to others, we open ourselves up to self-doubt. And if we let our doubter take over, it's not long before we feel resentful, frustrated and discontented with ourselves.

Envy isn't bad; it's a natural emotion. It's the way in which we react to envy that affects our self esteem and our relationships with others. There's a big difference between the friendly competition envy can encourage and the one-upmanship and revenge it breeds if not controlled. Competition makes us strive harder to learn from another's success. But using the emotion in a negative way to denigrate another can permanently damage relationships.

That's what happened to Robin, a thirty-six-year-old insurance salesman, who became so covetous of a colleague's success that he sabotaged his friend's deals by luring clients away with lower prices. The day his friend discovered what was happening was the last time the two men talked. And others, who heard about Robin's petty behavior, no longer referred clients to him.

Letting envy take control is one way to miss out on a lot of positive experiences. Sally was so envious of her friend's job as a theater manager that she refused to accept free tickets from her friend to attend a black tie fund-raiser, where she could have made the connections she needed to land a similar job.

Not allowing ourselves to learn from others because we're envious of their knowledge is self-defeating. Carl was delighted when his friend, Bob, offered to teach him computer programming in exchange for a few rides on Carl's catamaran. But after just one session at the computer, Carl became so angry that Bob knew so much more than he did that he enrolled in an expensive computer programming course and received little individual instruction.

Our sense of self-worth should not depend on how we measure up in comparison to others, but whether we remain true to our goals, live up to our potential, and create a life-style that meets our needs and desires. Sometimes, we envy another person's success without realizing all that person went through to achieve it. Before we decide that we want or deserve something another has, we have to ask ourselves if we're willing to make the necessary sacrifices to get it.

Tina was so envious when her friend, Midge, sold a novel she had written that she had to force herself to attend the book-signing party. Both women worked full-time at a university and had taken a fiction-writing class. For a year after they completed the course, Midge spent most evenings and weekends working on the novel she had started in class. Meanwhile, Tina kept her usual after-work schedule of shopping, watching television, and meeting friends for dinner, and she spent most weekends horseback riding.

Tina constantly complained about her lack of discipline and Midge's good fortune, until her boyfriend asked her if she was willing to give up all that Midge had to sell a manuscript. "I wanted the glory, but I wasn't willing to put in the time," says Tina. "To me, having evenings free to unwind from work, and riding and grooming my horse on weekends are perfect ways to spend my free time. I was envious of Midge's novel but not of the amount of work she had to do to get it published. I guess you can't have one without the other."

Before you let your doubter surround you with feelings of envy, separate reality from fantasy. Ask yourself:

Do you really want to be doing the things other people are doing?

Are you willing to make the commitment?

What makes you feel good?

Are you trying to prove something to some body?

Can you concentrate on improving your strong points?

Are you feeling guilty because you know you haven't put in the time you should have?

Once you decide what you want and what you're willing to do to get it, let your reinforcer help you develop a plan to move toward your goals. You can learn from a friend's accomplishments. Analyze the steps your friend took to reach his goal and apply some of those steps to devise your own plan. Did your friend get a new and exciting job by taking evening seminars, attending the right social functions, or getting the help of an employment agency? But be sure to use your friend's road to success as a source of inspiration, not imitation. Don't become a clone. Others will see through the disguise, and you could hurt a friendship. Let your reinforcer create new approaches that are uniquely yours.

It's natural to feel envious at times. But just as with other negative messages our doubter sends us, we have to recognize the source of our envy and confront it so that it doesn't control our lives.

If being around someone you envy makes you feel bad or causes you to say or do things you'll regret, consider spending less time with that person until you are able to work on your self-confidence. Avoiding the person may seem cowardly, but it might be the only way you can begin to concentrate on your strengths and not on your weaknesses.

If your envy has hurt a friendship, you may want to admit your feelings. Consider apologizing for not showing as much enthusiasm for your friend's success as the occasion warranted. Simply admit that you were feeling inadequate or that you wished you could have done as well. Chances are your friend will understand and may point out characteristics you have that he or she has always admired.

Your reinforcer can help you trust yourself and your abilities. Don't let your doubter waste your time by comparing you to others. Instead, use that time to create your own success.

JEALOUSY: A MONSTER OF A SLIGHTLY DIFFERENT BREED

There's a fine line between the definition of envy and jealousy. According to Robert Bringle, Ph.D., associate professor of psychology at Purdue University at Indianapolis, while envy is a feeling of dissatisfaction with ourselves in comparison to others, jealousy is a fear that something we have will be taken away.[7] Most of us think of jealousy as the hurt, betrayal, or rejection we feel when a lover's attention has started to drift to someone else. But you can also feel jealous when a friend, a boss, a parent, or someone else you're close to seems to be paying less attention to you and more attention to someone else.

The extent to which you feel jealous can often be linked to your childhood. If your parents continually told you that you weren't good enough or compared you to others, you probably feel jealous as an adult more often than the person who was highly esteemed as a child.

Social psychologists who have studied jealously have shown a link between romantic jealousy and self-esteem. A study conducted by Dr. Bringle of 144 men and women showed that the incidence of jealousy is related to the level of self-respect. Those people who were jealous the most often and most intensely had less positive self-esteem.[8]

Dr. Bringle's research indicated that jealous people are much more dissatisfied with life and feel that the world is controlling them. Often they are more dependent on their partners for feeling of self-worth. They see themselves as inadequate and fear losing someone in their lives who makes them feel loved and needed.

Jealousy, like envy, can shroud you with self-doubt if not dealt with immediately. If you feel that someone or something is stealing another's love away from you, try to determine if the feeling is justified. Ask yourself the following questions to see if your jealousy may stem from problems you're having in other areas of your life:

Are you bored with your job?

Are the children getting on your nerves?

Do you lack friends or hobbies to keep you busy?

Are you angry for another, unrelated reason at the person whom you feel is vying for your place in a relationship?

Are you seeing what could be a platonic friendship as something romantic?

If you're sure your jealousy is justified, deal with it appropriately. Don't do something that you'll regret or that may harm your partner's respect for you. A little jealousy in a love relationship can make you try harder and prevent you from taking a relationship for granted. And your partner may even try to make you jealous so that you'll give him or her extra attention. Are there little things you can do to demonstrate your love? Can you spend less time away from home? Can you plan an evening out for just the two of you?

Another way to handle jealous feelings is to talk about them with a friend or relative whom you can trust to keep your conversation confidential. In a safe environment you can express your anger and frustration and use your reinforcer to help you determine what steps need to be taken. And you will probably be relieved when your friend tells you that he, too, has had the same type of feelings.

Finally, evaluate your relationship with the person whose affection you're afraid of losing:

Do the two of you communicate well?

Do you support one another emotionally?

Have you been taking each other for granted?

Are you relying too much on that one person to fill all your needs?

If your feelings of jealousy are toward a lover, have you discussed the boundaries of your relationship or are you just assuming that you both think alike? Your partner may think that having friends of the opposite sex is fine while you might consider it a threat to the relationship.

Once you've identified the true source of your feelings and have developed some creative ways to approach them, you may want to talk to your partner. Try to remain calm and avoid making accusations. If you want someone to love you, you must show him or her that you're worth being loved.

9

ALCOHOLISM, DRUG ABUSE, WEIGHT GAIN: THE SYMPTOMS OR THE CAUSE?

WHEN self-confidence doesn't come from within, people often try to find it through external means. They may use drugs, alcohol, food, sex, work, loud and aggressive behavior, and even books, television, and movies to escape from feelings of self-doubt.

Most people who try to find refuge from their doubts instead of confronting them find only temporary relief. It may take weeks, months, or even years, but many eventually realize that they can't avoid their problems forever. When they finally come to that realization, they often have even more problems to solve. Self-doubt causes them to run from their problems, but running away or turning to addictive behavior creates additional obstacles and new doubts to overcome. An alcoholic's job may be threatened, an overeater's health may be jeopardized, a workaholic's marriage may suffer, a drug abuser may face legal consequences.

When you don't believe you're good enough, it's natural to look for ways to make yourself feel better. But don't get caught trying to hide from self-doubt. Recognize when you've gone past the point of brief indulgence and your behavior has become compulsive. The man who can't limit the number of martinis he drinks after work, the woman who finds herself eating a piece of cake but can't remember making the decision to eat it, and the teenager who can't function without taking a few pills are people who have lost control over their behavior and are acting compulsively. If you depend on someone or something to make you feel good, it's time to evaluate your behavior and consider alternatives.

ALCOHOL AND PILLS PROVIDE LITTLE REFUGE

Most of us know people who can't loosen up until they've had a few drinks. One of the most common reasons people drink is that alcohol makes them feel good by reducing their normal inhibitions. Alcohol is a depressant. Like a tranquilizer, it relaxes people and helps to alleviate feelings of pain, guilt, and personal inadequacy.

Brian never goes to a party without having had a couple of drinks to help him suppress feelings of inferiority. By the time he has had a few more drinks at the party, he says and does things he would never say or do if he were sober. He makes a fool of himself in front of people he respects and whose respect he wants and damages important relationships, but still he continues to use alcohol instead of facing the sources of his insecurity.

Thirty-two-year-old Ellen can make love only when she's intoxicated. The alcohol helps her to reduce feelings of inhibition that stem from her teenage years when her parents told her that sex was wrong and dirty. The next morning, Ellen rarely remembers her sexual experiences, so she's constantly searching for sexual satisfaction.

Dave feels incompetent at work. He spends his lunch hour in a bar. By the time he returns to his office, he has a false sense of confidence and is very competitive. Lately he's been coming into work later and taking lunch earlier—he can only function after a few drinks.

People use alcohol to help them feel comfortable in uncomfortable situations and to overcome feelings of pain or inadequacy. "When life seems overwhelming, people do things to try to block out the pain and mitigate bad feelings," explains Kay Shirley, M.S.W., co-founder of FACT (Family Alcoholism Consultants Team) in New York City. "What better way is there to sedate bad feelings than with a drug. Alcohol temporarily eases the pressure."

At first, one or two drinks may make a person feel good, but slowly the drinker needs more and more alcohol to overcome feelings of doubt. And while he may have started drinking to feel comfortable in certain situations or to overcome a traumatic experience (the break-up of a marriage, the loss of a job), he soon begins to feel the need to drink more and more, until he is psychologically and physiologically addicted.

"I counseled a woman who was raped," says Steven F. Bucky, Ph.D., Clinical Director of Alcohol and Drug Treatment Services at Mission Bay Hospital in San Diego, California, and who was formerly responsible for evaluating the U.S. Navy's alcohol and drug treatment programs throughout the world. "She had never drunk before, but one night after the rape, she bought a beer to calm her nerves. That drink made her feel good, so she drank a case of beer the same night. Several years later, when I began seeing her, she was drinking a case of beer and a bottle of vodka every evening."

Like those who turn to alcohol, people who start using drugs to overcome doubts find that, as time goes on, they need increasing quantities of the drug to produce the desired effect. Today, cocaine, similar to an amphetamine (speed), is one of the most widely-used drugs and one of which addicts can never seem to get enough.

"Cocaine users get a sudden euphoric feeling, but when they come down, they frequently feel sad and alone," explains Dr. Bucky. "That's why so many people use as much coke as they have available at one time—whether that's 50 or 500 worth of the drug. When the cocaine wears off, they feel depressed, so many turn to alcohol and develop a dual addiction, or they look for ways to find money to buy more cocaine, and that often leads to criminal behavior."

The *only* way for a person who has turned to alcohol or drugs to confront self-doubt is, first, to overcome the addiction and, second, to work on self-esteem. "It's virtually imposssible to build a person's self-confidence while he's being torn apart by alcohol or drugs," Dr. Bucky says. "As the alcoholism interferes with his life, the alcoholic or drug abuser frequently feels bad that he cannot control himself. The more out of control he feels, the more self-doubt he experiences. Most alcohol and drug abusers think they can stop whenever they want to. The realization that they can't is often devastating."

Few alcoholics and drug abusers simply wake up one morning with the sudden urge to stop their addictive behavior. The abuser needs to be convinced to change and that often means pressure from family, an employer, a physician, or the legal system. But it takes considerable commitment to stop drinking or using drugs because once a person stops the addiction, he has to admit that his behavior has caused pain to himself and others. And he must begin to confront his doubts, instead of running away from them.

The most effective way for alcohol and drug abusers to begin overcoming their addictions and addressing their problems is through professional counseling. For severe problems, in-patient hospital programs for alcoholism or drug addiction treatment are available. For less serious addictions, Alcoholics Anonymous meetings, out-patient hospital programs, county clinics, and group and individual therapy offered by psychologists, psychiatrists, social workers, and counselors are available. Your family physician or school counselor should know the type of resources available in your community.

"Ridding the body of alcohol is easy—detoxification takes only about eighteen hours. The biggest struggle the alcoholic faces is getting rid of self-doubt," says Kay Shirley. "Building up a person's self-esteem is the major thrust of alcoholism and drug treatment programs because recovering addicts know that they have failed in their personal relationships and in their jobs. Treatment programs are designed to help people gain the self-confidence they may have never felt and to go on without depending on alcohol or drugs. We help people to see that they are worthwhile."

Shirley teaches the families of recovering alcoholics that while they too are powerless over alcohol, they are not powerless over themselves. "You can control what happens to you by the choices and decisions you make," Shirley says. "If one decision doesn't work, you have the power to make another choice. People can control their own lives to an incredible degree."

When the drinking or drug-taking stops, addicted people who are trying to rebuild their self-esteem must often modify their relationships. "They have to accept that many of their relationships have changed or been destroyed and understand that it may be necessary to end others," explains Bucky. "The support of friends and family is crucial. Alcoholics and drug abusers need to be able to forgive themselves, and they need as much emotional support as possible to do that and to overcome the addiction.

"One thing recovering substance abusers can do is to picture what they were like before they became addicted," Bucky offers. "They need to realize that they had a distorted self-image and that they really do have worth and value."

Fifteen years ago, television and movie personality Dick Clark began drinking to cope with the break-up of his marriage. "I was on television during the day hopefully exhibiting my wonderful, warm personality, but at night I was trying to bury my depression with alcohol," says Clark. "Finally I realized that I had to take the bitter with the sweet and to go on with life. I was lucky because I was not predisposed to the disease of alcoholism, and it was easy for me to stop drinking heavily.

"Some people who have had an addiction or a problem that has caused their self-esteem to suffer say that they can't go on," Clark continues. "But unless you have an untreatable physical illness, there's no reason why you can't make a comfortable life for yourself. You can be depressed over the loss of a child or mate, sad about the death of a friend, or mad about a bad business deal, but you must continue with life. You do have a choice. You get back from life what you put into it.

"One of the most important lessons to be learned in life is that if we fail, we must start again," states Clark. "I am a survivor in a business that is based on a high mortality rate because I always have a dozen projects going at all times. If one is a smashing success, great, but if one fizzles, I bury it as quickly as I can and go on to the next.

"Setting new goals keeps life interesting," believes Clark. "Every few weeks, I run a little appraisal of my life. I say, 'Hey, I was going to do so-and-so, or maybe I ought to do such-and-such.' What I'm really doing is dangling a carrot in front of my nose. Some people can sit back and be content, but I find that very unsatisfying. To me, persistence and perseverance are the keys to personal satisfaction and success."

OVEREATING: THE UNSIGHTLY COVER-UP

Just like the alcoholic and drug abuser, other people turn to food when they feel lonely, frustrated, insecure, bored, or dissatisfied. Overeaters try to fill voids in their lives with food. Many overweight people use their fat as a shield to protect them from experiences they perceive as frightening. If you use food to try to escape problems, ask yourself:

What benefits do you get from the food?

Do the benefits outweigh the negative effects?

How long does food provide an escape from your problems?

Does being overweight make you feel strong, important, or dominant?

Is the extra weight an excuse for not expressing your sexuality?

Does the weight or the amount of food you eat bring you extra attention?

Ron kept on twenty-five extra pounds to protect his marriage. "I was afraid that if I lost weight I would start having affairs," he says.

Dina decided that if she were fifty to seventy pounds overweight, she would have the prefect excuse not to go out and find a job once her kids were all in school. "I can't go out and find a job looking like this," she says.

Alice gained weight to spite her husband. "Fat really turns

him off, so by being overweight, I can deny him sex," she admits. "I know he doesn't like making love to me when I'm fat."

Are you putting on weight to punish someone—your parents, your spouse, your boss?

For years, Paula's husband asked her to lose weight but it wasn't until they separated that she lost fifty pounds. "Being out on my own made me realize that I had always tried to lose weight to please someone else," says Paula.

"That's the same way I felt when I was in grade school," Paula remembers. "I didn't have many friends, so I tried to do things that would make other kids like me. I guess I got tired of trying to please everyone else, so when Gerry asked me to lose weight for him, I rebelled."

If you overeat out of anger, frustration, disappointment or fear, analyze your behavior and your needs. The next time you reach for a candy bar just an hour after lunch, ask yourself, "Why?" What do you really need? Maybe you're angry about the way your mother talked to you on the phone. Instead of devouring the chocolate bar, which will only make you feel guilty later, call your mother and tell her how hurt you were by what she said. Try to discuss your feelings rationally so that you can resolve the problem. Even if you and your mother don't agree, praise yourself for taking constructive action. But don't use food as a reward. Find another way to make yourself feel good. Treat yourself to a walk in the park, a manicure, or a long-distance phone call to a friend.

If your mother or father used food as an escape, you may too. Some parents may encourage a child to eat fattening foods because it gives them an excuse to indulge. A mom who makes cookies for her kids has a perfect opportunity to pop several into her mouth as she lifts them off the baking sheet and into the cookie jar. And food is often used as a reward—a way to say, "I love you."

How was food used in your family? Was it a reward for a job well done? Or a bribe to get you to do something you disliked? Were you punished if you didn't clean your plate?

Use the 10-step plan to identify your doubts and help you understand why you eat the way you do. You probably learned at an early age to use food to control doubt and pain. Once you know why your doubter encourages you to eat, you can turn to your reinforcer to create new ways to approach feelings of uncertainty. You have to believe that you have the power to change before you can make the change. Once you develop a sense of well-being and believe that you can cope with feelings in a healthier way, you will become better able to control what you eat.

OTHER ESCAPE MECHANISMS

If only we could be as creative in trying to overcome self-doubt as we are in trying to escape from it. People devise amazing ways to avoid confronting their feelings, from spending their days at the race track, to diving into their work, to sleeping excessively.

If you are ruining your life—or if someone you know is ruining his—by trying to escape from problems or fears instead of confronting them, it is time to seek help. It is time to learn how to trust yourself and discover better ways to cope with problems. But don't expect to do it alone. You'll need the love and support of your family or friends, and probably you'll need professional assistance.

10

Be All You Can Be—Conquering The Fear Of Failure And The Fear Of Success

WHETHER it's winning a tennis match, soaking up the applause after a dazzling stage performance, earning top dollar on a sales force, or hearing a compliment from a friend, most of us want to succeed. Each of us has his own definition of success, but we all know it when we feel it: it is that sweet sensation that we've accomplished what we set out to achieve.

To many of us, success doesn't come nearly as often as we'd like. But what gets in our way more than any other obstacle is not our opponent, stage director, sales manager, or a jealous friend; it's our own insecurities.

Self-doubt holds us back from attaining our goals in two seemingly different, yet profoundly similar, ways—by the fear of failure *and* the fear of success. Both are dangerous traps that can keep us from trying and ultimately from succeeding, no matter how big or how small the goal.

FIGHTING THE FEAR OF FAILURE

It's easy to understand the rationale behind the fear of failure. No one really wants to fail. Even the smart-alecky kid who is kicked out of class seeks recognition, whether to impress his peers or to win his parents' attention. And when his suspension from school sends his father's blood pressure to the boiling point, he's gotten his attention and attained his goal.

Not wanting to fail—that instinct to escape impending disaster—is often a great motivator. It encourages us to get to work on time, prompts us to obey traffic rules, and is the reason that we expend so much energy to beat our whiz kid nephew in a game of chess.

But at the other extreme, the fear of failure and the criticism that may follow can also freeze us into taking no action at all. Many people avoid testing their talent because, to them, no recognition is better than negative reaction. But what kind of fulfillment can there be if we always avoid taking risks? Not only do we safely escape criticism, judgment, and controversy, but we miss out on opportunities to grow, excel, and feel good about ourselves. Playing it safe can only be a ticket to a boring, frustrating life.

There are many excuses people make for not trying, a number of which seem perfectly acceptable on the surface. We blame our hectic work schedule, the kids' piano lessons, or our spouse's demands. But more often than not, we could make our way around obstacles and take a chance if we didn't subconsciously question our ability to succeed.

Frustrated with her job as an accounts-receivable clerk for a large manufacturing firm, Laura wanted to return to school and earn a master's degree in business administration. Before she could begin school, however, she was required to take a graduate entrance exam. Laura put off buying the book to prepare for the exam until the weekend before the test. She crammed for the exam, but by Monday morning she knew she wasn't ready and put it off for another semester.

It took a lot of prodding, but Laura finally admitted that she was afraid of failing the entrance test. By not buying the book in time to adequately prepare for the test, she had created a perfect excuse to put off taking the exam. But another six months in the same boring job and new insights on how to confront a challenging situation gave Laura the inspiration she needed to attempt the test.

"Now, before I give in to the fear of failure, I ask myself, 'What's the worst that can happen?'" says Laura. "Even if I don't pass the test, I'll be no worse off than I am right now."

Like Laura, many people who fear failure are terrified of confronting their limits. By not trying at all, they never know how much they can't do, but they also never know how much more they can do, either. They don't give themselves a chance to reach their potential; they spend their lives frustrated by undiscovered talent.

The fear of being rejected is another reason that people quit trying. It hurts when we are unable to attain our goal, but one failure does not doom you to a lifetime of disappointment. If we can learn from our mistakes and have the determination to try again, success may be waiting around the corner.

David is a forty-year-old model who has learned that being rejected today doesn't mean that tomorrow won't hold better fortune. "Modeling is a profession filled with rejection," he says. "Models are constantly getting turned down for jobs because they don't 'look' the part. If you're not careful, you can take that kind of rejection personally. I've had to realize that if I'm not selected for a particular modeling job, it's not because I'm not a good model but because my looks or qualifications don't meet their specific needs at that time—but I might be just what they're looking for next week."

If you have been hurt by rejection or paralyzed by the fear of failure, here are a few steps that may help you:

Admit your feelings. Avoid making excuses for not trying and, instead, make a list of your fears. Ask yourself: Are you afraid of what others will think of you if you fail? Do you think you'll make a fool of yourself if you try and don't succeed? Why do others' opinions matter so much?

What's the worst that can happen? Ask yourself this question before you decide not to try. Even if you don't succeed, will you be any worse off than you are right now? Maybe your ego will be bruised or you'll realize that you need more experience, but will you really lose anything? Chances are you'll walk away from the experience with a lot more knowledge, a bundle of insight, and new determination to try harder next time.

Set attainable goals. You're less likely to fail if you start small and work your way up. Instead of not writing at all because your style isn't that of The New Yorker, try selling your articles to local and regional magazines. You'll gain the experience and the confidence to move on to bigger markets.

Get the support of a friend. We often fear teasing and ridicule more than failure itself. If you're uncomfortable in a certain situation, ask a friend to support you. For instance, if you want to try out for a role in the Shakespeare festival, find out if a friend has similar aspirations. At least see if someone will help you learn your lines and accompany you to the audition. With someone to cheer us on, it's often easier to try.

What's important to you? Success may mean something different to you than to your wife, your father, or your best friend. When you try to live up to another person's expectations, it's easy to become anxious about failing. Ultimately, we do a better job at something we're interested in. Be honest with yourself, family, and friends about what you want to achieve. The pressure we feel from other people to succeed is often more overwhelming than the pressure we put on ourselves. In a kind way, let others know when they're placing demands on you to do something you really don't want to do.

What can I learn from this experience? If you've been turned down for a job or your work has received less than glowing reviews, you know how easy it would be to decide that you'll never try again. But instead of giving up hope, use that experience to help you identify how you could improve yourself or your work, and then with that new knowledge, try again. Chances are you will improve tremendously.

COMBATTING THE FEAR OF SUCCESS

Have you ever known someone who talked and talked about achieving something and then, when the goal came within reach, quit trying or became distracted by something that suddenly assumed more importance? That kind of behavior is indicative of a person who is afraid of succeeding.

At first glance it seems absurd to want something and then sabotage your chances of getting it. But when you examine the consequences of success, it's easy to understand why one person may be just as afraid of success as another can be of failure. Success results from high achievement and just the pressure of having to maintain that level of achievement is enough to make a person not want to try.

"The higher you climb, the greater the fall," is the way Dave saw success. "After I quit singing in a band I worked with for years, I spent months looking for work as a soloist. Just as I was about to break into a very good nightclub, I decided to take a job as an airline steward. When I'm honest with myself, I know that I avoided the singing job because I was afraid of what my friends expected of me after all those years of me telling them what a great solo performer I would be."

According to a 1977 study by Matina Horner, Ph.D., president of Radcliffe College, performance is inhibited when a person feels that serious consequences will result from the success. That type of fear is more prevalent in women who are trained as young girls to believe that femininity and high achievement are mutually exclusive.

Horner says that a woman who strives to succeed has it doubly hard. If she fails, she doesn't live up to her own standards; if she succeeds, she may think that she'll be unpopular, unmarriageable, and lonely.

Renee, the mother of three children, competed for a higher paying position within her company. She wanted the job, but because she would be a manager, she knew it would take more than forty hours a week. She'd be expected to attend evening board meetings and occasionally travel out of town. If she took the job, she'd have to forego some of her responsibilities at home. "There'd be fewer gourmet meals, less time to help the kids with schoolwork, and almost no time to volunteer at our favorite charity," she said. "I worry that my family will love me less if I take this job."

Success brings with it a fear of the unknown. We can never know how others will react—or even how we'll react—to something we have not yet done. Some people worry that their egos will inflate if they get what they want. Others are afraid that family and friends will expect continued success and are afraid they will let people down. And there is always the possibility that others may become envious and relationships will be damaged.

Guilt is another reason that people dodge success. They feel that they don't deserve success because they haven't worked hard enough or because they aren't good enough. Some who succeed once attribute their success to luck and tell themselves that they'll never be able to do that well again.

If you've abandoned your dreams because of the fear of success, here are some questions to help you identify and resolve your fears:

> What impact will success have on my relationships with my spouse, children, boss, colleagues, friends, and relatives?
>
> What other demands will be made of me, and do I want to assume that responsibility? Will I be expected to work more hours? Will I have more people making demands on my time?
>
> Can I maintain that level of success? How will I feel if I can't? Will I allow myself to make mistakes?
>
> Whom will I please if I am not successful? (Did your parents tell you as a child that women could not succeed in business? Did your father tell you that you couldn't achieve more than he did?)
>
> What changes will take place in my life if I'm successful and which changes do I fear? (If a new job will mean you will have to travel, are you afraid of being alone or are you afraid that your family won't know how to fend for itself?)
>
> If I do not take the steps I need to succeed, will my frustration manifest itself later? (Will you be hostile to those you felt held you back? Will you not be as giving to others?)
>
> If I do succeed, will I expect others to treat me differently? What if they don't?
>
> What will I be doing a year from now if I don't work toward the goal I set?
>
> Will I regret my decision? Will I be able to redefine my goals?

Once you've answered these questions and thought about your answers, determine if your perceptions of success are realistic or if they have been biased by fear. Then write yourself a permission slip to succeed that begins, "It is okay for me to..." Putting things down in words may give you the impetus you need to begin working toward a goal.

In addition to the permission slip, write a brief outline of what you'll need to do to achieve your goal. Answer these few questions in your outline:

What do I want and why?

What is the first step I'll need to take to get there?

What are other important steps I'll have to take?

What will be the benefits of my success?

How will my success change my life?

Success is only worth the price if we feel worthy of the honor and if we can enjoy the feeling of accomplishment. You must believe in yourself and in what you are doing. Realize that everyone deserves success, and when it comes your way, be willing to be recognized for it.

BE ALL YOU CAN BE

There's no such thing as luck. Success occurs when you're prepared to take advantage of opportunity. You must be willing to work toward your goals. Persistence is one of the most treasured traits of success-oriented people. Author Madeleine L'Engle personifies determination. L'Engle had sold several books before age thirty, but for the next twelve years sold only two.

"On my 40th birthday, I was waiting for a letter from a publisher on a book that was very close to being accepted," says L'Engle. "My husband called me from the post office and told me the book had been rejected. I took that as the ultimate message that I was supposed to give up writing and learn how to scrub floors and bake pies. I covered my typewriter in a great gesture of renunciation and was walking up and down my office bawling my head off when I suddenly stopped in my tracks. My subconscious mind had developed an idea for a novel on failure. I uncovered my typewriter and began writing again."

"That night," L'Engle continues, "I wrote in my journal, 'I'm a writer. That's who I am, even if I'm never published again.'"

L'Engle didn't sell the book on failure, and she received between twenty-five and thirty rejections on another book, A Wrinkle in Time, before it sold. "After you've received that many rejections, it's easy to doubt yourself," the author says. Finally the publishing house of Farrar, Straus & Giroux decided to buy *A Wrinkle in Time,* but they told me, 'Now dear, we don't want you to be disappointed. This book is not going to sell. Children can't possibly read it. We're just doing it as a sort of self-indulgence because we love it.'"

And the public loved it, too. *A Wrinkle In Time* has been read by millions of children and adults throughout the world, and it earned an American Library Association Newbery Medal for children's literature. Soon the book will be made into a motion picture produced by Norman Lear. By refusing to give in to failure, L'Engle created her own Cinderella story . . . and so can you.

AFTERWORD

Now that you have seen how others have conquered their doubts and you have learned to use the 10-step plan, you can begin to overcome the doubts in your life. Remember that the doubter within you has value. It has protected you and kept you safe, but it has also limited you and caused you to fall short of your goals.

We can never get rid of the doubting side of our personalities, nor would we want to. We need the doubter to keep us in balance, but even more important, we need to develop the creative side of ourselves—the reinforcer.

By recognizing that your doubter was created at a very young age, and understanding how you've nourished it throughout the years, you can use the 10-step plan to confront your doubts in the future. Your reinforcer has the power to help you keep self-doubt in perspective so that you can harvest your positive energy.

When you feel self-doubt taking hold of you, stop and review your personal 10-step plan for a happier and more successful life:

STEP 1
IDENTIFY YOUR SELF-DOUBT

What has been bothering you?

Describe your self-doubt.

STEP 2
THINK BACK TO WHEN YOUR DOUBTS BEGAN

Determine when your doubt was planted.

Recreate an early experience of self-doubt.

STEP 3
PICTURE YOUR DOUBTING SIDE

Create a mental image for your "doubter" and give it a name.

STEP 4
THANK YOUR DOUBTER

Your doubter has helped you. Describe how.

STEP 5
DO YOU REALLY WANT TO CHANGE?

You must be ready to have your doubter play a less significant part in your life or your doubter may find excuses for you not to change.

STEP 6
PICTURE YOUR CREATIVE SIDE

Develop an image for your "reinforcer" and give it a name.

STEP 7
CHANGE NEGATIVE MESSAGES TO POSITIVE ONES

Think of two or three "gifts" or positive messages that your reinforcer can give you when doubt begins to surface.

STEP 8
LET YOUR REINFORCER EDIT THE PAST

Determine how your reinforcer could have handled situations in the past when you were troubled by self-doubt, how it could have worked with—not against—your doubter.

STEP 9
USE YOUR CREATIVE STRATEGY TO CONQUER DOUBT

Let your reinforcer work on your present doubts.

STEP 10
CREATE THE FUTURE YOU WANT

Put your reinforcer to work whenever your doubter begins to overshadow you. Now that you are aware of the effect your doubter has had on your life, you can use your reinforcer to balance your doubter and create new alternatives and experiences. You have the resources to live your life the way you want it to be!

In Chapter 1, you took the C.Q. Quiz to determine your level of self-doubt. Now that you have read this book and begun to apply its ten steps to your life, take the quiz again. I believe you will be surprised at the difference in your scores.

C.Q. QUIZ

QUESTION	OFTEN	SOMETIMES	NEVER
Do I feel inferior to others?			
Do I think I'm wrong before I consider that someone else might be?			
Do I think others are talking about me?			
Do I worry about whether or not others like me?			
Do I miss out on opportunities because I don't try?			

THE CONFIDENCE QUOTIENT

QUESTION	OFTEN	SOMETIMES	NEVER
Do I feel envious of a friend's accomplishments, but am I unwilling to test my own ability for fear I might fail?			
Does another's criticism threaten my feelings of self-confidence and worth?			
Do I avoid getting into new relationships for fear I'll be rejected?			
Do I eat, smoke, or drink alcohol excessively?			
Do I make excuses for myself?			
Do I have trouble accepting compliments?			
Do I question my social skills, my appearance, my wardrobe, and do I compare myself to others?			
Do I overcompensate for my insecurities with boisterous, boastful, forceful, or hostile behavior—or withdrawal?			

Was I right? What was the total of your "Often" or "Sometimes" responses at the beginning of the book?

What is it now?

If you follow the ten steps to conquer self-doubt that I have presented, I know that you will live a happier, richer, more fulfilling life. Good luck.

FOOTNOTES

1. Samuels, Mike, M.D. and Nancy, Seeing With the Mind's Eye: The History, Techniques and Uses of Visualization (New York, NY: Random House, 1975), xi.
2. C. Coleman, Ph.D., Abnormal Psychology and Modern Life. (Glenview, IL: Scott, Foresman, 1972), 250.
3. Ibid., 251.
4. Donald Lammers, "Relationships Between Perceptions of Self and Spouse, Marital Adjustments and the Negotiation of Conflict" (Ph.D. diss., University of Texas at Austin, 1979), 209.
5. Jewish Family Services of Metropolitan Detroit, "Money Myths in Marriage," Clinical Social Work Journal, (Spring 1978), 53-56.
6. Lammers, 208.
7. Robert Bringle, Ph.D., "Conceptualizing Jealousy as a Disposition," Alternative Lifestyles, vol. 4, no. 3., (August 1981), 276.
8. Ibid., 277.

INDEX

Addiction
  alcohol, 104-109
  drugs, 104-109
  overeating, 109-111
Adolescence, 91-92, 93
Agoraphobia, 53
Alcohol abuse, 104-109
Allen, Marcus, 86-87
Anxiety, 21-25
  housewives and, 52, 53
Arguments, marital, 79-80, 81-82

Behavior, negative, 6, 8
  alcohol and drug abuse, 104-109
  marriage and, 74-75
  overeating, 109-111
Bosses, dealing with, 67-69
Bringle, Dr. Robert, 99, 100
Bucky, Dr. Steven F., 106, 108

Careers, switching, 64-67
Change
  evaluating, 69-70
  fear of, 54, 64-67
Childhood, and self-image, 11-12, 15-16, 86-93
Choices, difficulty in making, 5
A Circle of Quiet, 55
Clark, Dick, 108-109
Cocaine, 106
Confidence, *see* Self-confidence
Counseling, alcohol and drug abuse, 107
Creativity, 33-40, 44-45
  self-discipline and, 98
Criticism, of self, 7, 52

Decision-making, 14, 69-70
Depression
  self-doubt and, 6, 7
  housewives and, 52, 53
Discipline
  creative, 98
  parental, 93
Dissatisfaction
  controlling feelings of, 5-6
  envy and, 96-99
Divorce, 81, 83-84
"Doubters," 28-33
Doubt, *see* Self-doubt
Drinking, *see* Alcohol abuse
Drug abuse, 104-109

Empty nest syndrome, 59-61
Envy, 96-101

FACT (Family Alcoholism Consultants Team), 105
Failure, fear of, 37, 39, 40, 114-117
Fatigue, 52
Fear, 21-25
  of change, 54, 64-67
  of failure, 37, 39, 40, 114-117
  of rejection, 116
  of success, 40, 117-120
Guilt, 54, 118-119

Homemakers, and self-doubt, *see* Housewife syndrome
Horner, Dr. Matina, 118
Housewife syndrome, 50-51
  empty nest syndrome, 59-61
  motherhood and, 58-59
  neurasthenia and, 51-55
  overcoming, 55-58, 61-62
Housework, and marriage, 72, 74
Hypochondria, 52

Illness, psychosomatic, 52
Infancy, and self-image, 10-11
Instincts, trusting, 70

Jealousy, 96-101
Job satisfaction, 64-70

L'Engle, Madeleine, 55, 120-121

Marriage, 72-75, 84
  arguments and, 79-81
  money and, 79-80
  parenting and, 78-79
  possessiveness and, 75-77
  self-esteen and, 77-78
  sex and, 80-81
Motherhood, 58-59
  empty nest syndrome, 59-61

Neurasthenia
  housewives and, 51-55
  job-related, 64

Overachieving, 12-13
Overeating, 53, 109-111

Parenting
  effective, 86-93
  marriage and, 78-79
Parents, effect of, 10-17, 86-93
Personality reinforcement, 20, 33-40, 54-55
Phobias, 53
Possessiveness, 75-77
Psychosomatic illness, 52

Reinforcement, personality, 20, 33-40, 54-55
Rejection, fear of, 116
Relationships, establishing healthy, 13-14, 15
Routines, changing daily, 55-57, 64

Self-confidence, 46, 104
  housewives and, 50-62
  job change and, 64-70
  parents and, 10-17, 86-93
  self-doubt and, 1-8, 20-48
Self-discipline, 98
Self-doubt, 2-4, 10
  adolescence and, 91-92, 93

alcohol abuse and, 104-109
dissatisfaction and, 5-6
divorce and, 81, 83-84
drug abuse and, 104-109
envy and, 96-101
fear of failure, 114-117
fear of success, 40, 117-120
housewife syndrome, 50-62
jealousy and, 96-101
job-related, 64-70
marriage and, 72-82, 84
negative behavior, 6, 8
overcoming, 8, 14-17, 20-48, 122-125
overeating and, 109-111
parents and, 11-17, 86-93
past experiences and, 25-28, 40-43
positive aspects of, 6
self-criticism and, 7
Self-esteem, 7, 8
  alcohol abuse and, 104-109
  childhood and, 89
  drug abuse and, 104-109
  envy and, 96-97
  infancy and, 10
  jealousy and, 100
  marriage and, 77-78
  overeating and, 109-111
Self-image, 5, 15
  childhood and, 11-12, 15-16, 86-93
  infancy and, 10
Sex, 104, 105
  marriage and, 80-81
Shirley, Kay, 105, 107
Success
  attainment of, 120-121
  fear of, 40, 117-120

Therapy, 13
  alcohol and drug abuse, 107

Worth, see Self-esteem; Self-image
A Wrinkle in Time, 121

World Almanac Publications Order Form

Quantity	ISBN	Title/Author	Unit Price	Total
	31655-X	Abracadabra! Magic and Other Tricks/Lewis	$5.95/$7.95 in Canada	
	32836-1	Africa Review 1986/Green	$24.95/$33.95 in Canada	
	32834-5	Asia & Pacific Review 1986/Green	$24.95/$33.95 in Canada	
	32632-6	Ask Shagg™/Guren	$4.95/$6.50 in Canada	
	32189-8	Big Book of Kids' Lists, The/Choron	$8.95/$11.95 in Canada	
	31033-0	Civil War Almanac, The/Bowman	$10.95/$14.75 in Canada	
	31503-0	Collector's Guide to New England, The/Bowles and Bowles	$7.95/$10.95 in Canada	
	31651-7	Complete Dr. Salk: An A-to-Z Guide to Raising Your Child, The/Salk	$8.95/$11.50 in Canada	
	32662-8	Confidence Quotient: 10 Steps to Conquer Self-Doubt, The/ Gellman and Gage	$7.95/$10.75 in Canada	
	32627-X	Cut Your Own Taxes and Save 1986/Metz and Kess	$3.95	
	31628-2	Dieter's Almanac, The/Berland	$7.95/$10.25 in Canada	
	32835-3	Europe Review 1986/Green	$24.95/$33.95 in Canada	
	32190-1	Fire! Prevention: Protection: Escape/Cantor	$3.95/$4.95 in Canada	
	32192-8	For the Record: Women in Sports/Markel and Brooks	$8.95/$11.95 in Canada	
	32624-5	How I Photograph Wildlife and Nature/Rue	$9.95/$13.50 in Canada	
	31709-2	How to Talk Money/Crowe	$7.95/$10.25 in Canada	
	32629-6	I Do: How to Choose Your Mate and Have a Happy Marriage/ Eysenck and Kelly	$8.95	
	32660-1	Kids' World Almanac of Records and Facts, The/ McLoone-Basta and Siegel	$4.95	
	32837-X	Latin America & Caribbean Review 1986/Green	$24.95/$33.95 in Canada	
	32838-8	Middle East Review 1986/Green	$24.95/$33.95 in Canada	
	31652-5	Moonlighting with Your Personal Computer/Waxman	$7.95/$10.75 in Canada	
	32193-6	National Directory of Addresses and Telephone Numbers ,The/Sites	$24.95/$33.95 in Canada	
	31034-9	Omni Future Almanac, The/Weil	$8.95/$11.95 in Canada	
	32623-7	Pop Sixties: A Personal and Irreverent Guide, The/Edelstein	$8.95/$11.95 in Canada	
	32624-5	Singles Almanac, The/Ullman	$8.95/$11.95 in Canada	
	31492-1	Social Security and You: What's New, What's True/Kingson	$2.95	
	0-915106-19-1	Synopsis of the Law of Libel and the Right of Privacy/Sanford	$1.95	
		Twentieth Century: An Almanac, The/Ferrell		
	31708-4	Hardcover	$24.95/$33.95 in Canada	
	32630-X	Paperback	$12.95/$17.50 in Canada	
	32631-8	Vietnam War: An Almanac, The/Bowman	$24.95/$33.95 in Canada	
	32188-X	Where to Sell Anything and Everything/Hyman	$8.95/$11.95 in Canada	
	32659-8	World Almanac® & Book of Facts 1986, The/Lane	$5.95/$6.95 in Canada	
	32661-X	World Almanac Book of Inventions®, The/Giscard d'Estaing	$10.95/$14.75 in Canada	
	29775-X	World Almanac Book of World War II, The/Young	$10.95/$14.75 in Canada	
	0-911818-97-9	World Almanac Consumer Information Kit 1986, The	$2.50	
	32187-1	World Almanac Executive Appointment Book 1986, The	$17.95/$24.95 in Canada	
	32628-8	World Almanac Guide to Natural Foods, The/Ross	$8.95/$11.95 in Canada	
	32194-4	World Almanac's Puzzlink™/Considine	$2.95/$3.95 in Canada	
	32626-1	World Almanac's Puzzlink™ 2/Considine	$2.95/$3.95 in Canada	
	31654-1	World Almanac Real Puzzle™ Book, The/Rubin	$2.95/$3.95 in Canada	
	32191-X	World Almanac Real Puzzle Book 2, The/Rubin	$2.95/$3.95 in Canada	
	32625-3	World Almanac Real Puzzle™ Book 3, The/Rubin	$2.95/$3.95 in Canada	
		World of Information: see individual titles		

Mail order form to: **World Almanac Publications**
P.O. Box 984
Cincinnati, Ohio 45201

Orders must be prepaid by one of the following methods:
☐ Check or Money Order for _____ attached
☐ Bill my charge card (Add $5.00 processing charge for orders under $20.00)

Order Total _____

Ohio residents add 5.5% sales tax _____

Shipping and Handling: _____
(Add $2.50 for every purchase up to $50.00, and $1.00 for every $10.00 thereafter)

TOTAL PAYMENT _____

Visa Account #		Exp. Date
Master Card Account #		Exp. Date
Interbank #		Exp. Date
Authorized Signature		

Ship to:
Name _____
Street address _____
City/State/Zip Code _____
Special Instructions: _____

All orders will be shipped UPS unless otherwise instructed
We cannot ship C.O.D.